Journey to Freedom

Bobby Harrison

© Bobby Harrison 2008

Journey to Freedom

ISBN 978-0-9560065-0-9

Published by Freedom Publications
c/o 64 Herbert Road
Shoeburyness
Southend-on-Sea
Essex SS3 9JR

A CIP catalogue record of this book
can be obtained from the British Library.

Prepared for publication by Michael Walsh at
THE BETTER BOOK COMPANY

A division of
RPM Print & Design
2-3 Spur Road
Chichester
West Sussex
PO19 8PR

Cover picture – SNAFU (Bobby Harrison) at Reading Music
Festival – 1972. Picture from London Evening Standard

Journey to Freedom

From the height of fame in the music world to the
depths of despair with the drug scene and the darker
side of life, to becoming a born-again Christian, and
discovering the grace of God and the love of Jesus Christ.

The true story of Bobby Harrison
singer, songwriter, and musician
from the original Procol Harum group

DEDICATED TO

My daughter Julia and my late brother Richard Harrison
Also to my road managers, Keith, Larry, Jo and Bruno.

My late brother Richard

MY PRAYER

Lord Jesus Christ
I am sorry for the things I have done wrong in my life.
I ask your forgiveness and turn from
everything I now know to be wrong.
Thank you for dying on the cross for me
to set me free from my sins.
Please come into my life and fill me with
your Holy Spirit and be with me forever.
Thank you Lord Jesus,
Amen.

ACKNOWLEDGEMENTS

This book covers my life and the journey which led to me to becoming a Christian. I would like to thank all the people who have helped me and encouraged me along the way, especially:-

Graham Bannister, Pete Wilson and the band 'Journey' and a special thank you to Mark Churchward and Dave Cooke. Lastly my friends Irene and Stew, for all their work in the co-writing and editing of this book. Thanks to Malcolm and Judy.

CONTENTS

CHAPTER ONE

WHERE LIFE BEGINS

My devoted mother and myself 1940

Where life begins and the journey commences, as it did at 12.30 a.m. on the 22nd June 1939 in East Ham Maternity Hospital, a boy for Mr and Mrs Harrison. I was wrapped in a shawl and placed in a crib. My mother said I cried a lullaby of my own and tapped my tiny toes even then when I was just a few hours old – it was wind I imagine!

I was christened Robert Leslie Harrison and after a few days was taken home to Park Avenue in East Ham. I was the first child in the family and it was just at the start of the Second World War. Soon everyone would be busy constructing Anderson shelters in their gardens and food was to be rationed. Fathers were called up and peoples' lives were changed big-time due to the Second World War.

East Ham was not safe from air raids, being close to London and the river Thames so I was sent with my sister, Yvonne, who had arrived shortly after me, to Worcester. Things were not so good there but there was no threat of bombs and according to my memory the bacon was exceptional – the smell sticks in my mind to this day!

We did not stay in Worcester for the entire duration of the war as, probably like most mothers with babies, my mother wanted us to come home, so we returned to the family home. My mother had two more children, Michael and Christine who sadly both died not long after they were born. This was not unusual in those days as things were hard.

Later we moved to 37 Brooks Avenue and my sister Susan was born, followed shortly by my other sister, Joan. Then we moved again, this time to Telham Road, off Bonnie Downs, East Ham; the type of house with an outside toilet and no bathroom springs to mind. I remember the pub on the corner, the Drum and Monkey. My mate Bobby Batt and I used to kick a ball up against the wall there.

The first school I attended was Vicarage Lane, in East Ham and then St. Michael's which was run by nuns.

My mother was a devout Catholic and an extremely clean lady. She would scrub everything and I can remember hating bath times (nothing unusual there – most young boys hate washing!) which were a once a week ritual. Out would come the tin bath in the kitchen and everyone took turns.

The nuns used the cane quite freely, as did most schools in those days – "whacking" is the word we used.

Another thing that comes to mind was one particular day when a rather large girl named Pat, who could only have been six years old, decided to take me into the girls' toilets and show me her secret bodily parts. Unfortunately curiosity killed the cat as I was caught red handed and paid for it in front of the whole school at dinnertime, with the cane on the tips of my fingers. It really hurt.

I shall never forget seeing a doodlebug for the first time while playing in the school playground. To a small boy it looked massive, about the size of a house – suddenly a silence and then the loud bang as it exploded near to the school. I stood shivering with shock and then I heard the sound of running feet – all the mothers were coming to take their children home. The White Horse public house, which was nearby, had been hit.

At the end of the war I found it difficult when my father came home. Also, my sister and I wondered who this strange man was, sharing Mummy's bed where we usually slept.

My father brought home with him an orange, which was a very exotic fruit in those days. Not many people had seen an orange let alone tasted one. It was cautiously peeled, sniffed and broken into segments to be shared amongst the family so everyone could taste a bit. This obviously made a lasting impression as later I was to use a picture of an orange on the sleeve of my first solo album called "Funkist".

The next school was St Bonaventure's which had no nuns, just a few monks about. Somehow though, I managed to get myself expelled. Like most small boys about that age, I made a dart with a pen nib and a milk straw. It must have been pretty good as the school decided they were not going to have any missiles today and I had to go but before going I was given the cane, six of the best on my bare bum.

Another school was found in Napier Road and later a newer school called 'Sir Thomas Letherby' [sic]. Here I met Peter Braybrook who played an important part in my young life as he introduced me to football. Peter was two years older than me and later played for Chelsea, West Ham and even went on to play for England.

I excelled at football and went on to be discovered by Malcolm Allison, who was manager at West Ham United and scout for West Ham Colts. I was only twelve when he signed me up and I used to attend training two or three times a week with matches at the weekend. Later I went on to play in the reserves for West Ham.

My father used to get jealous of my success and would pass comments such as "Go out and get ten pounds of spuds in your school cap", just piss-taking all the time because my mother was proud of me. All I ever wanted was for him to love me and I learnt at a very young age to ignore these sarcastic remarks. In a way it made me even more determined to be successful.

During my teenage years I enjoyed another sport, boxing, which was important to me at this time and I became East Ham schoolboy champion at my weight for two years running. I was now fourteen and would attend training classes at the back of the police station in East Ham twice a week with Police Sergeant Craddock. I remember sometimes seeing him on his police horse around town.

I won every fight at this young tender age and until I went into the army to do my National Service.

Cricket was also another sport I played and again I must have been pretty good as I was chosen to represent East Ham and Essex.

When I was fourteen, the family moved to Brentwood, to the appropriately named East Ham Council Estate. I finished my schooling at East Ham though, travelling by train from Brentwood each day.

The house we lived in was new and modern. It had three floors and four bedrooms, much better accommodation for us as a family. At the age of fifteen I left school to become a welder's apprentice with my uncle's firm in Barking. It was during this time I met David Bailey through a football mate called Danny. We would hang about together and would often go to the famous Flamingo Club and listen to Zoot Money, Georgie Fame and Eric Burdon and the Animals.

I began to be interested in the music scene and in particular the drums so I started to take lessons. Once a week I would travel to Sloane Square to my music teacher, Max Abrams, where I studied for four years. Max Abrams was an excellent drum teacher. He played with the likes of Sid Phillips, Jack Parnell and Ted Heath.

My parents bought me my first set of drums when I was seventeen, for twenty-five pounds. It wasn't long after that we fell out with the neighbours because of the noise. There were no sound-proof garages to practice in and most houses were terraced like ours, so you can understand why the neighbours got grumpy. However, this did not stop me as I had to practice.

With all the sport and music interest I never found time for the usual youth clubs or school dances. I was much too busy for these events, until one day, playing football in the reserves for West Ham, I broke my left arm in a match at Walthamstow and this was the turning point. I decided to leave the sporting world behind and concentrate on my music.

The music world was so good at this time with so many new ideas and plenty of venues. It was a great time to be young; an explosion of new rhythms and sounds; the start of Rock'n'Roll with Bill Haley and his Comets and Elvis Presley together with the big dance bands; the kind of music which only happens rarely over a period of time and it was so great to be a part of it. I could see there were even more opportunities and I didn't want to miss out on any of them.

Looming in the distance though, was my National Service. I wasn't really looking forward to it but there was nothing I could do to avoid it so like a lot of young men in those days, I had to leave home and join up for two years compulsory service for my country.

CHAPTER TWO

NATIONAL SERVICE

Band of the Royal Inniskilling Fusiliers – Drummer Harrison 1960

I had, at this time, just become engaged to my girlfriend Margaret so it was a very sad day when I had to say goodbye and travel by train on my own to Northern Ireland to join my regiment, the Royal Ulster Rifles Light Infantry. Then it was on to the Royal Inniskilling Fusiliers who were stationed at Omagh, and nicknamed 'The Skins'.

At first I hated it, especially the Corporal, who was in charge of me. Being a bit iof a rebel, after having had enough of the Corporal's arrogant manner and the way he shouted at me with his face right up close, I decided it was time for revenge. So at the end of one day I reached up to the top of his locker where the Corporal kept his helmet and I urinated in it without any hesitation. In the morning when we were getting ready for parade the Corporal reached up to get his helmet and of course was well and truly soaked in my bodily waters. After a great deal of swearing and shouting, the squad were told to line up and then the question was raised as to who did it? Of course no one stepped forward to admit it. Then the whole squad were threatened with being put on jankers which would have meant everyone cleaning the toilets with toothbrushes and then scrubbing their teeth with the same brushes. I couldn't let that happen so I owned up and was taken to spend the night in the cells. I was woken at five the next morning and was made to put on a full pack and climb over the assault course until I collapsed.

Things were sometimes very tough in the army. I will never forget a young man who was shot by the IRA. He was guarding the armoury when this awful incident took place. They got away with all the weapons and ammunition, which the young man was guarding at the time. This brought all of us more together and good friends were made during these times.

Because of my musical talents, I was chosen to play the drums in the band. This helped me to carry on learning to read music and kept my interest going. I was moved about during my two-year stint and remember being stationed in Dusseldorf, Germany for six weeks.

One evening I spent drinking in the town centre with the lads and managed to miss the last truck back to the barracks. This led to disaster as I was then declared a deserter. This meant I was picked up by the Military Police and locked up in the cells for a few days. Needless to say the assault course with the full pack was to follow again but by now, I was very fit.

After the six weeks in Germany were up, a two-week leave was given. This was the only leave to be granted in the whole two years, before joining a troop ship called the 'Devonshire', and heading for Africa. The journey would take about five weeks to reach Kenya, stopping at Malta and then passing through the Suez Canal, stopping at Port Said.

I remember the poverty and shock at a land with such little respect for life and in particular for their children, as they would even cripple their own child in order for them to beg for survival. They would wrap sticks round their little legs to stop them growing properly and maim them for life. It has left a lasting impression on me and I am sure the other young soldiers who can remember to this day the haunting look on those little children's faces.

While in Suez, the troop ship would sometimes be met with a barrage of small boats called bum-boats which were selling all sorts of items to the troops via buckets and ropes hauled up the side of the ship because we were not allowed to go ashore.

After the Suez Canal it was on to Kenya via the Indian Ocean to Mombasa where we landed and we went our separate ways. The ship went off to be scrapped and we went by train to Nairobi and then on to where we were to be stationed, at Nakuru. We had to travel past the Aberdare mountains by Lake Naivasha, to a town called Gilgil.

Another regiment called the King's African Rifles joined us ~~and~~ there and, as with every camp, the first job to be done was to dig the latrines!

I spent a year in Africa in which I played football for the army and we won all that was going. The team was also sent to Uganda to play on a small tour and everyone was surprised by the apparent wealth of the black people there, who were driving around in big cars, compared to the whites who seemed poor. The African and Indians wore no shoes when they played football but could hit the ball better than anyone. Of course I was still studying music with the band and boxed for the army at every opportunity.

On another occasion 'The Skins' were given the Freedom of the City of Nairobi. This was because of earlier problems with the Mau-Mau uprising, an awful time for the white farmers, but the army had acted as a security police force and this was their reward.

The camp was situated in a beautiful spot near the lake which was the home for the local flamingos and after a while, when we had settled in, some leave was granted. As with all young men, women were very much on our minds but we were told "No black women". This was like a red rag to a bull and together with two other mates, I went drinking at a local bar and very soon we were pretty drunk. It was not long before a man, who it turned out later was the local pimp, approached us and offered to take us to a camp full of young women. Well it was too much for us three young men to refuse such an offer with promises of young flesh so we quickly hopped into his vehicle and he drove us to a village somewhere nearby where there were two mud huts. We had no idea exactly where we were as it was dark. After alighting, the man told us it was five shillings for sex and if we wanted his daughter for smoke and talk it was half a crown.

There was only one room in the hut and I was second in line but I could not go ahead as I had something else on my mind. I had a dreadful feeling that we were in great danger because between us we did not have enough money. The man was getting agitated and suddenly pulled a machete out from somewhere and threatened us. The three of us were out of there so quick that the man had hardly time to blink. We were soon running through the dark countryside as fast as our army boots could carry us, dancing like kangaroos through the long grass, clutching our most valuable bits. Fortunately, as luck would have it, we somehow managed to find our way back to a main road and followed this to reach the camp safely. The training had obviously paid off but after this we all agreed we would drink at another bar in future!

On another occasion there was a plague of locusts and I was caught in this when going back to my billet. It was like being hit with a thousand darts all going bump, bump all over the place. It lasted about an hour and a half and after the loud humming noise had subsided, everyone went outside to see the aftermath. There was not a blade of grass or any leaves left anywhere. They had all gone.

At that time I had a little pet chameleon which lived in my mosquito net. He would sway and change colour, depending on the surrounding colour. He had his own little shelf by the bed and sometimes I would take him, in my pocket, for a walk. I'd find the right spot and watch him catch flies. After a few months of course I had to let him go which was a difficult thing to do as I had become very attached to the little fellow.

It was about a year later that I found myself on my way home to England on a large plane with four prop engines, stopping first at Malta with a days rest and then on to Stansted. Looking back on the whole experience, it was really quite enjoyable. Although I had been dreading it, the friends I made then are friends for life and are very special. I still ring my friend Malcolm who was in the army football team with me and now lives near Rochdale. We still visit each other.

CHAPTER THREE

A PROFESSIONAL MUSICIAN

Like most young men who had experienced two years away from home travelling the world with the army, I found it difficult to settle down and in the first year I had thirteen different jobs. My romance with Margaret broke up even though we had been engaged and I was totally spaced out. I had been brainwashed in the army and now had to adapt to everyday life in Essex.

Fortunately I had my music and this helped me through this difficult time. My music teacher suggested that I should apply for a job in Butlins, Skegness and to my delight I was accepted to play in the big dance band.

Whilst there, I met Ringo Starr who used to wear plenty of rings, hence the name Ringo. He was playing in a rock band called Rory Storm & the Hurricanes, from Liverpool and we would have a full English breakfast together each morning (as drummers do) in the staff canteen. Ringo of course left Butlins to go and join a group called The Beatles. The next time I saw him, he was on television singing and playing 'Love me do' which made me even more determined to succeed.

At Butlins, my accommodation consisted of a caravan which I had to share with another musician, a gay bass player. He made my life so intolerable that when my new girlfriend, Dorothy, came to visit me, I decided to return with her, back home to my parent's house.

Back home I busied myself with two jobs as my father was giving me plenty of ear-bashing with remarks like "You will never earn a good living playing the drums" and "You will have to give it up when you get older". I smile now as I have proved you could play until you were ninety! Sadly my father hasn't changed one bit towards me or my success over the years. Because of my faith now, I have even tried, until recently, to get on with him but it seems this will not be possible. I fear that time is running out and there is nothing I can do. At least I have tried.

During the day I drove for a Danish Bacon Company and in the evenings I played in various groups. I was beginning to model my singing on my favourite musicians, James Brown, Ray Charles, Wilson Pickett, and Little Richard; they were my idols.

I joined a group called 'The Jimmy Riche Combo' who were from the East End and I played the drums in the band. My new girlfriend, Dorothy, would come and listen when I was playing. The bass player, the late Alan Spenner, was only fourteen at the time and he went on to play with "Joe Cocker and the Grease Band.

Another local band I played in at this time was called 'The Rockerfellas', based in Brentwood.

Eventually I decided to form the first band of my own called "Golden Apples of the Sun". David Bailey, who had become famous for his photography, and Andrew Loog Oldham, the Rolling Stones manager, acted as our managers and David came up with the name for the group from a book. We went on to record a single called "Monkey Time".

Another evening job I had was to sing in a group called 'The Powerpack' at 'The Plough and Harrow' in Leytonstone High Street. We recorded two singles and were backed by the famous jazz player Ronnie Scott.

I also recorded my own record about this time, a cover version of Bobby Hebb's 'Sunny', on CBS Records with Ronnie Scott on saxophone.

Phil Jacobs owned the pub we played in, and the famous Kray brothers were involved somewhere. Lammy, Phil's brother, used to keep a crow bar under the counter just in case! The pub would be full of dodgy people and there would be frequent fights. The East End was full of gangs and 'loveable rogues' who thieved – real East-Enders. If they liked you they would do anything for you. I was learning fast about life, people and their struggles. It was life in the raw. It was the beginning of 'the journey'.

I worked five nights a week, and it was a great learning platform, and where I did all my ground work in the music industry.

I, together with other musicians, would often sit in on river trips up the Thames with the likes of Cliff Richard & the Shadows and many others. This is how I came to ring Gary Brooker one day to ask him if he would be interested in joining my group and to my surprise Gary thought I was calling about the vacancy for a drummer with his group, 'Procol Harum'. The group had previously worked under the name of 'The Paramounts' and I had met them in Southend on many occasions at a coffee bar called 'Shades', owned by Robin Trower's father. Robin, was an exceptional guitar player in 'The Paramounts' and later went to the United States and made it big time. He also played in 'Procol Harum' after Ray Royer left.

So, after meeting with Gary and hearing the demo tape, I decided this was an excellent opportunity. 'Procol Harum' already had a recording contract and it would be well worth travelling to the south London church for an audition. It seemed an opportunity not to be missed, so I arranged to have a couple of days off and drove down with my drum kit and my best mate at the time, Georgie Gibbs.

There had been forty other candidates for the job but as fate would have it Gary liked my work and immediately took me on. I had plenty of experience and had developed a style that was exactly what was needed for the group so the next three months were spent rehearsing, in the church of all places!

My journey was now to take a new direction and I had no hesitation in deciding to give up my day job driving for the Danish Bacon Company and also the evening sessions singing and playing the drums in the East End pub. I had become a professional musician again and despite my father not being happy about my choice, I felt something was driving me on. I just had to follow this gut feeling. This proved to be the right decision as the group went on to be an overnight success and reach the top of the charts.

While we were still rehearsing, the group's producer, Denny Cordell, was under pressure from Tony Hall, a DJ for BBC radio, to release "A whiter shade of pale", written by Gary and lyricist, Keith Reid. Tony wanted to play the record on his programme as he felt it was special. In the end Tony won and it was played for the first time.

The reaction was awesome which proved the song was going places and it was suggested and agreed to release it within two weeks so it was rushed into production.

The rest is history as it was an instant hit and went straight to number one for six weeks, one of the biggest hits of the 1967 'summer of love'.

CHAPTER FOUR

PROCOL HARUM

Number one in the charts – Top of the Pops – May 1967

"A Whiter Shade of Pale"

Strangely, I found this a very frightening experience as things were happening so quickly. I was not used to the professional music scene and suddenly we were mixing with famous people and living the high life. We were invited everywhere and appeared on 'Top of the Pops', with Dusty Springfield on the same bill. She had always been one of my favourite singers and now I was performing on the same programme as her.

Suddenly the group did not know what day it was. Our feet did not touch the ground. It was a very nervous time for me. There was no home life – it was hotels from now on with a schedule of bookings, appointments, shows and tours in the making.

We were bumping into the Beatles and the Rolling Stones who were doing the same shows as us. The record was released on the Continent and was an immediate hit in Holland, Belgium, Germany and France, in the latter, being in the charts for a year at number one.

One of these shows, in August 1967, was with Jimi Hendrix at the Saville Theatre and to my horror Paul McCartney was in the audience with John Lennon. Later, when we met up, John told us he liked our record very much and played it often.

One of my girlfriends at this time was Sue, from Texas, a girlfriend of Monika Danneman. Monika was Jimi Hendrix' girlfriend and on a few occasions we had the unfortunate task of taking her to hospital when she'd had too much alcohol or drugs. A couple of years later, after Jimi's tragic death, Sue and I would visit Monika to comfort her at the apartment which she used to share with Jimi.

Sadly, Monika never really got over losing Jimi and later went on to take an overdose herself, from which she never recovered. This may have helped me later, when I had a wake up call after taking too much bad stuff myself.

'Procol Harum's' image and appearance were extremely important and as London was the top place in the fashion scene, there was only one place to shop for some new outfits so it was off to Kings Road in Chelsea to see what we could find. As we were just going into one of the best shops in the

Kings Road we met The Beatles coming out. They wished us luck and this was just one of those shopping expeditions we were often on.

It was life in the fast lane. There were interviews for the newspapers and the media, and appearances on television. It was like entering a different time zone. It was mind blowing. It was hard to keep up with emotions. We were young and keen but had not had time to settle down and reflect on what we had achieved. It was like being in a race. We were only getting four hours sleep a night and I was getting extra pressure coming from my family.

There were drug dealers hanging around every corner and it is easy to see how we, as young men, were tempted to take either pills to perk us up before performances or sleeping pills to help us sleep after a hectic night. There was always plenty of weed to smoke and alcohol to drink, which was surrounding our new lifestyle.

Along with all this there were certain women, nicknamed 'groupies', who would throw themselves at us at every opportunity, offering their bodies for sexual pleasures. The sixties were the era for free love and it was available along with all the other temptations for rock stars. I found this quite frightening at times and had mixed feelings about the women as I had been brought up a good Catholic boy but my ego had gone through the roof and I was nearly out of control.

It was Denny Cordell, the producer at the time, who offered me my first drag on a cigarette of dope but the hard drugs were to follow later. The journey, on the slippery slope to disaster, was beginning.

CHAPTER FIVE

FREEDOM

Walt Monaghan (Bass), Roger Saunders (Guitar), and myself (Drums)

With all the stardom and bright lights of show business came also the seedy side: the hangers-on; the crooks and the easily available drugs and alcohol; the women who let the band know in no uncertain circumstances that they were available in ones, twos and more. They did not mince their words – it was as simple as "What do you like for breakfast?" or simply "f*** me"!

The pressure to perform and record another hit was immense and so 'Homburg' was recorded and released as soon as possible. It was not such a big hit as 'A whiter shade of pale' but reached number four none-the-less and some people even preferred it. It also reached the top twenty in the States so after our tour of Europe, preparation for America was on the cards.

This first six months was like an atomic explosion and it was taking its toll on everyone. Life was very hectic travelling and performing without any rest.

Tony Secunda arrived on the scene and Denny Cordell, Procol Harum's producer, created between them a lot of friction. A takeover was in the air and big time crooks were hovering around. I did not want the take-over to happen and neither did Ray Royer. We liked things the way they were being managed by Jonathan Weston, our original manager, whose family was in the film industry.

But like a lot of things in life, change has to happen and so I decided to split and Ray came with me to form our own group called 'Freedom'. At first I had to make sure that royalties due to me and to Ray from Procol Harum, were secure and this meant going to court. Just at the last moment it was fortunately all settled out of court which made good reading in the newspapers who managed to get hold of the story. Sometimes there is a happy ending.

Now with 'Freedom' the first job was to find a bass player and keyboard player so an advert was placed and eventually Steve Shirley was chosen for bass and Mike Lease for keyboards.

Very soon our first job offer came, not only to write and play the music for a film, but also to appear in it. The film was called 'Nerosubianco' (Black on White) produced and directed by two Italians, Dino De Laurentiis and Tinto Brass.

This was to be the ultimate in publicity exposure for 'Freedom' as we were to appear in the nude, with only the instruments keeping our modesty hidden. It was good publicity even though we were actually wearing underpants!

We appeared in the film playing the songs as a commentary, without any dialogue. In its original format it was a hundred minutes long, but has since been edited to sixty. There were a total of fourteen songs which were written and recorded at Olympic Studios in London, all in just two months. Elton John came in to hear us while this was being recorded. He was recording his first album at the time and he was quite impressed.

An album was also produced called "Black on White" but was lost for some years. It has since been found and is now a collector's item. Even the members of 'Freedom' were not aware of the album's existence until recently, when we were approached in connection with its current release by Angel Air. We thought we had just written a film score.

The film was considered to be a bit risqué in its day and was probably always destined to be an art film although it was critically acclaimed at the Cannes Film Festival.

Other than at Cannes, the film did not get very well received and soon afterwards, Dino became unpopular with the Italian Inland Revenue and had to leave the country in a hurry. He later became a successful director in Hollywood producing 'King Kong' and 'Flash Gordon'.

The meaning of 'Black on White' was taboo. It simply meant a black man and a white woman as lovers. It seems ridiculous now but at the time there was so much prejudice around. It just goes to show us how far we have come in the last forty years.

There is a famous picture of 'Freedom' printed in the Sunday Times, a double spread, showing the group playing in the nude. Nudity was not uncommon strangely enough but black and white couples were and, dare I say it, frowned upon. It seems very strange today, looking back.

Afterwards, when the film was finished, everyone was invited out to Dino's villa in Monte Carlo and this included the band who were to play at Dino's daughter's twenty-first birthday party. The villa was in the most fabulous beautiful setting and was more like a mansion than a villa, with large grounds, palm trees and a large yacht moored where the garden gently sloped down to the Mediterranean Sea.

It was a grand finish to all the work we had accomplished in making the film, but there were changes yet again on the horizon.

I was becoming more interested in 'the blues' while Ray was becoming interested in Scientology and it was causing friction. Ray had been hard work before this and now he was getting into Scientology, it made things much more difficult. He was becoming strange and I struggled to communicate with him so I took the sad decision to ask him to leave.

It was not long before Roger Saunders and Walt Monaghan, who were friends at the time, agreed to join Freedom and a new manager too was not far away.

CHAPTER SIX

NEMS

Earliest photographs of the original Procol Harem line up.

Left to right:- Ray, Gary, me, Dave and Matthew.

I arranged for the new 'Freedom' to have a regular gig in the Bridge House pub in Canning Town to get the band sorted. We had started to pack them in when the management company 'NEMS' came to hear us and liked us so much they signed us up immediately. 'NEMS' also managed 'Black Sabbath' and 'Yes'.

In the early days we would be paid weekly and would collect our wages from our manager's office. On one such Friday we were greeted with the front door bursting open and a guy ran in and kicked the office door in and tried to stab the manager. It turned out he was a debt collector and this concerned us as it was our first pay cheque. We were worried if we had done the right thing but things turned out alright after this frightening start. There was talk about some tours but first they sent us to Majorca for a month to write a new album. I was taking drugs big-time now, nearly every day. It was so easy to get. Everyone knew where to go to get some and most were taking something.

Cocaine was purchased, usually in rock form. This way you knew it was pure and not tampered with. It would have silver chips in it and a piece about the size of a thick penny would cost the equivalent of two hundred pounds today. Once purchased it would be carefully ground down and divided into two halves, then quarters and three small packages would be carefully wrapped individually in white paper like butchers' paper, to keep it dry. These three would be used later. The remainder would be divided into two, making a line of each portion of powder. A crisp twenty pound note would be carefully rolled up and used to sniff one portion whilst holding the other nostril closed. The other white line would also be drawn up the twenty-pound note in turn.

The result would be instant, the feeling of extreme confidence, as if you can take on the world and achieve everything you could possibly want. There would be nothing to stop you. Nothing would be in your way. You felt like a king. If there were any females around you would be so enhanced it could make an erection last for hours and the age and appearance of the woman or women would not be considered, as the world was such a beautiful place. The overriding feeling of the drug simply blotted out all the usual desires of love and union. It was a slippery slope into the darker side of life.

Later, it was a slow descent back to the real world and would leave you with a feeling of great exhaustion so a Valium would be taken, to aid the return to some sort of normality, plus of course the alcohol. It was abuse of the body and I knew this – deep down inside I was not happy.

I was beginning to hate the way my life was going with the drug scene and the groupies but I was young and it seemed an amazing experience despite the down side, which was coming down after the drugs.

On one of our mini tours in Germany, when we had played in about eight or nine clubs, we were coming home, which is always the worse part of the trip as everyone is slowly coming back to reality after having had such a good time. We had travelled in our own transporter which had all the gear and everything we needed in it, including seats for us. We had stopped for the night at a café which was a hotel as well. Roger Fennings, who was second in command to the tour manager, was always bitching like an old tart. I had just about had enough of his constant bitching and did play rather a nasty prank on him.

We were having coffee when he was called away to the telephone and this was my opportunity so I pissed in his remaining cup of coffee. To my horror when he returned he drank it and it had no immediate effect, except I felt disgusted with myself. It was about a year later when he was leaving that I told him what I had done and apologised. He went mad!

A tour of the USA was next on the agenda, supporting 'Jethro Tull' for about six weeks on the east coast. It had been nicknamed the 'United Sex of America', which was not too far from the truth. There were the usual drugs and orgies with increasing bad behaviour which was almost expected of us. This particular tour was made all the more interesting as 'Jethro Tull's Ian Anderson was interested in aviation and had organised a private aircraft to ferry us around on our tour, visiting all the venues in style.

It was not the private jet you would expect to see today, which greeted us parked on the apron, but an older aircraft with two propeller engines, which was looking slightly well used. There were two groups on board, together with their roadies and the usual entourage which are needed to set up the equipment. Ian sat up the front with the pilot and I sat with Roger (the late Roger Saunders, my guitar player in 'Freedom' at the time).

It was a special day. The weather was good, which was essential as we were to fly over Niagara Falls. Everyone was sitting back enjoying the view when disaster struck. The window next to me suddenly became covered in black oil and the engine was making plenty of unusual noises, sounding like someone had dropped their tool box into it. Roger looked at me and we both had the same thought – that we were not going to get out of there alive.

The aircraft swerved violently and Niagara Falls looked like it was coming up to meet us. We both began to pray and the Lord's Prayer was the first prayer we both thought of at the same time. It seemed like eternity before Ian left the flight deck and came back into the cabin to inform everyone that we had lost an engine but everything was under control. We were able to continue on one engine and managed to land at the nearest airfield, Buffalo.

The next day we returned to the airport and had to board the same aircraft again, which had been repaired by now.

Everyone was very subdued on that and the next few flights until we regained our confidence in the aircraft. It seemed it was not our time to go just yet and I was thankful. I felt my prayer had been answered and someone was looking after me. Roger simply blamed Ian for hiring a cheap aircraft as he was a Scot.

The tour was exhausting with the flying and setting up for sound checks at 4 p.m. each day, followed by the performance and the late nights mixed with the drugs, alcohol and women. There were no days off and, as this was at the height of 'Jethro Tull's career, their performances were mind blowing. It was another world.

CHAPTER SEVEN

FUNKIST

My First Solo Album

On return from our tour with 'Jethro Tull', I was totally spaced out. I was drained of energy with lack of sleep, too many drugs and bad things, despite having had a wonderful time. I needed time to unwind and adjust, time to visit my family and wind down. Now it was back to reality in the UK.

Two months were spent recording and song-writing before the next tour with 'Black Sabbath'. Music was

35

changing to heavy rock which stirred the audiences into a kind of frenzy and was awesome and shocking. 'Black Sabbath's number one was called 'Paranoid', which gives an idea of what it was all about. It seemed all self-respect had gone and to be shocking was the only way to express the move with the times. 'Black Sabbath' were good, very good but on and off the stage, bad stories made good reading. What else could they shock us with? Things were going from bad to worse in this respect.

'Freedom' toured Europe, visiting Germany, France and the Netherlands, as well as the United Kingdom, together with 'Black Sabbath' and 'Curved Air', a group, with a female lead singer. The concerts were all sold out and a huge success. We did plenty of crazy things together and plenty of drugs every day. Our confidence could not get any higher, with thousands of adoring fans applauding and cheering us on stage every night. Our egos were through the roof once again and we were as high as could be.

In one particular concert in Holland, couples who seemed to be spaced out on drugs were having sex in the toilets. It was the darker side of life which was never far away and I felt very unhappy with it. I knew that one day, if I didn't get out, there would be a sticky ending.

Another degrading episode involved excrement being thrown from a car window at another car whilst we were travelling from one gig to another. Fortunately the receiving car's window was shut and the poor victim was spared. For legal reasons, I can't name the famous rebel/person responsible but I thought that animals were better behaved!

At another venue we were staying in a very good hotel when trousers were dropped in the dining room to shock the other guests who were having dinner at the time.

I was not happy with this side of things but had to go along with it as it was all around me. I also knew I was abusing my body but I was totally hooked on drugs by now and dependent on them. I was discovering that life was not always so good at the top.

After this tour had ended, I stayed at home for a while to try and come back to the real world. I would sometimes envy people with relationships and often wished I could be like them.

Groups are like a family when working together for long periods of time, living out of each others pockets. The first two years are good but in the third year the interest begins to wane and the group usually splits, as it did with us.

After 'Freedom' broke up, I did not know quite what to do. Then a chance came for me to record with an American company for a solo album called 'Funkist'. The material had basically been written for 'Freedom' but I had started to move in a different direction and I wanted to get away from the usual and 'funk' was happening. So together with some great rock legends it was recorded and the management were really enthusiastic about the end product.

Bringing together a group of top quality players can work out well – or can be a disaster! I was lead vocalist and played drums. Others were all in famous bands:-

Micky Moody (guitar) was a master of the slide guitar and played on numerous hits during the seventies.

Matthew Fisher (keyboards) played the organ part on 'A whiter shade of pale' and had created a whole new approach to the Hammond organ – more about this talented writer, singer and producer will make the headlines later.

Chris Stewart (bass guitar) played with practically everyone in the music scene at this time, from Joe Cocker to Spooky Tooth.

Walt Monaghan (bass guitar) was a solid distinctive bass player and was with me in 'Freedom'.

Clem Cattini (drums) started with 'The Tornados' and later became one of the best session players ever.

Herbie Flowers (bass guitar) was an original member of 'Blue Mink' and also played with 'T Rex'.

Bob Sargent (keyboards) was a well-known keyboard player and also worked as a producer.

Tony Iommi (guitar) was 'Black Sabbath's guitarist and had known me through touring together.

Henry McCulloch (guitar) was a member of 'The Grease Band' and 'Eire Apparent' and later with Paul McCartney's 'Wings'.

Ray Owen (vocals) was vocalist with 'Juicy Lucy'.

Ian Paice (drums) was best known for his many years with 'Deep Purple' and today with Paul McCartney's new group.

'Funkist' was not released at the time of recording, but held back for later. It was already to go and the management thought it was a good product but suddenly, when they heard a whisper that I was getting a new band together, they decided to put the album on hold and wait and see the new band before releasing it.

'Long Gone' is perhaps my favourite track on the entire album. I wrote the lyric for it, and it's all about going on tour. It's one of those Rock'n'Roll tour songs I suppose and was eventually released as a single.

The new emerging band was called, 'SNAFU' and we signed a deal with 'World Wide Records', the mother company of 'NEMS'.

CHAPTER EIGHT

SNAFU

My first son Luke – Duck Quay Florida

Around this time, one of my favourite haunts was a famous club called The Speakeasy, in London. It was always full of stars and musicians and interesting people and it was there that I met Linda Lovejoy who changed my life once again as you will read later.

Linda was a petite young lady with frizzy hair and a ring in her nose. She had an outrageous personality and was quite a challenge for any man. She was American and had been adopted and brought up in the United States by Frank Lovejoy, the chairman of Kodak.

It was not long before I moved in with her at her flat in London. The landlady was Liz Wilmott, an artist who also worked in the film industry, making costumes.

Linda was ahead of the times. It was unusual for a woman to have a piercing anywhere other than her ears in those days and she also travelled a great deal. She made several trips with her girl-friend Robin, visiting Afghanistan, Turkey and Tibet. She would be quite secretive about these trips but eventually she was to confide in me and I was quite shocked at what she told me. In those days it was easy to pass through customs who were not so particular and somehow Linda always managed to pass through without any problems. This meant of course that there was always a good supply of 'getting high' to be had and meant also we had quite a turbulent relationship.

I was concerned for her safety and as time went on and we drew closer, she knew I was very concerned and wanted her to pack up that kind of life – which she eventually did.

Once Linda was caught up in Afghanistan while a war was on and she was unable to fly home until things died down which took quite a few months.

Being from a wealthy background Linda owned an apartment in Ibiza and sometimes we would both hang out there, when it suited us. I recall the toilet was a hole to pee through, about as big as a plate, in a concrete floor – no good if you had bad knees!

On one occasion Linda disappeared to Ibiza and I went after her only to find she was having an affair. We did get back together again and in fact decided to get married but one of the conditions was that I was to help smuggle her Tibetan Spaniel to England. His name was Tomna and he was sedated with sleeping pills and placed in a straw bag. This worked out fine, except that he kept passing wind all the way and I had to take the blame for this. The dog arrived home in the UK and awoke as if nothing had happened.

Soon after, Linda discovered she was pregnant. She had already lost two, one as she had German Measles and another was also terminated due to Hepatitis.

This time though, a boy was born and we called him Luke. I was already a father with a daughter, Louise, who had moved to Canada with her mother, Dorothy. We had lived together back in the days when I played in the East End and had split when 'Procol Harum' reached the big time. I felt very bad about this at the time as everything was happening so quickly. My father never understood why we had split and this led him to disown me in the end.

This time I was delighted and another child followed in eighteen months time, another boy, called Jake. Linda and I took both the boys on holiday between tours to her father's holiday home in the Florida Keys. I particularly remember one Christmas we had the most wonderful time in the sun and on Frank's large yacht. The sea was so blue and the water so clean. The beautiful colours in that part of the world are magical.

Luke and Jake now both live in London.

The new band, SNAFU, which had been forming since I met Linda, was a sought-after band and we were hoping to get a big hit. An album was put together and recorded at The Manor, Oxfordshire. It was the first to be recorded there, apart from 'Tubular Bells' which was recorded by Mike Oldfield about the same time. Mike was just finishing his famous album as SNAFU were just starting. The studio was owned by Richard Branson and was his very first business venture. The studio is still active today and is reputed to be Paul Weller's favourite recording studio.

Our keyboard player, Pete Solley, was asked to play violin on the Tubular Bells album by Mike Oldfield.

After recording the album, we toured the world promoting ourselves with 'Emerson Lake and Palmer', 'The Eagles', 'Doobie Brothers' and 'Joe Cocker and the Grease Band'. I was still on dope and cocaine as many of us were – it was all part of our lifestyle. Also, there was always the table of drinks laid on for us in the dressing room with every drink under the sun, all free of course.

All the concerts were sold out and a huge success. The equipment needed for these events was loaded on trucks and the drums alone for Carl Palmer needed one large eight wheeler truck. Usually we travelled by road and would be travelling for about two months at a time – not much sleep and sex in abundance, (three girls in one day would not be unusual) plus the alcohol, and a liquorice-all-sorts of drugs! On return, the after effects kicked in and it was time to chill out.

During this time we had a dispute with the management company and Patrick Meehan from NEMS, so a change of management was in line. I knew that 'Status Quo's

Management, Quarry Productions, were interested in taking on SNAFU so eventually, after discussions, we settled for them.

So another album was released and a couple of singles and then a tour of Europe with 'Status Quo'.

We were so sought-after by other bands as we were role models – even 'Status Quo' were a little jealous. We were so professional, had been on the road for ages, and were writing great songs. In fact it caused some bad feeling because we were going down better than them at some concerts. At the end of the last concert in Berlin, we pulled out all the stops, the crowd went berserk and gave us all such a rush, we became uncontrollable and damaged quite a lot of 'Status Quo's equipment, which made us unpopular. We have never been on their Christmas list since!

Even today, when I see my twelve-year-old stepdaughter's Bratz dolls, there is one there that reminds me of star-struck Parfitt and another that reminds me of three-cord Rossi. We could not stand being with squeaky-clean 'Status Quo' anymore. There were a few grumpy groaning undercurrents, hence, at the end of the tour, SNAFU were given our marching orders.

This all took about three years. The tours were taking their toll and I was tired and spaced out. Worse, we just could not get the hit we needed. It was for me to be described as the 'nearly man'.

The next tour was in the States. We were staying at a hotel in New York, Central Park, near the gig, so near we could walk to the venue. Smokes were offered and the group were smashed out of their minds.

45

Ray Charles was playing at the gig along with Emerson Lake and Palmer when I swear I saw sparks and fireworks jumping off the cymbals as I played and I ended up nearly falling of the stage. The next day I was taken to the airport in a wheelchair, as I could not walk. It was a wake-up call for me and the shock of it made me think very seriously about what I was doing to my body.

It was to be the last tour, as SNAFU decided enough was enough – it was the beginning of the end again. David Coverdale, who was forming 'White Snake' and had previously been with 'Deep Purple', spotted Micky Moody, my writing partner in SNAFU, and offered him good money which Micky could not refuse and so he went. As he could not be replaced, this really meant the end.

SNAFU had been my baby and I was very upset and disillusioned after Micky Moody left. I lost a lot of passion for the business and spent more time at home. This created arguments between Linda and me – a divorce was on the cards.

Inniskilling (Skins) Football Team circa 1960 – Bobby 2nd row 2nd right

BACK ROW (left to right): Leeming, Conway, Horsborough, Clark, Pendleton, Downie, Taylor, Frame, Cunningham, Gallagher, Fitzpatrick.
FRONT ROW (left to right): Warren, Lees, Roxburgh, Harrison, Morrissey.

47

Bobby with King's Africa Rifles chums - early 1960s

At "The Plough and Harrow" circa 1966

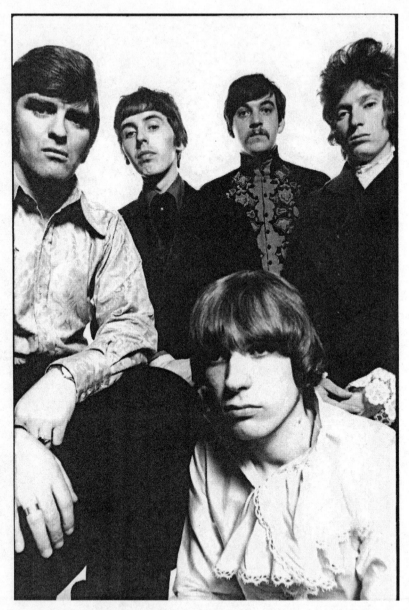

Procol Harum 1967

'SNAFU' taking a break circa 1972

Reg Isadore – loveable rogue

Sweating it out with Gus Isadore circa 1978

Iceland – Promoting Meatloaf circa 1988

Hallgrimskirkja Church, Reykjavik

Joey – Lead singer, 'Europe', with fans, circa 1988

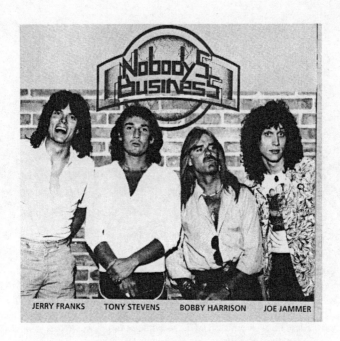

JERRY FRANKS   TONY STEVENS   BOBBY HARRISON   JOE JAMMER

Margret with my daughter, Sydney Harbour, circa 2005

Eldest daughter, (second left), Louise, with her family in Selfoss, Iceland.

My sweet little sisters – Joanie, Yvonne, and Susan

Wendy with Charlotte

'Journey'

Roger, Stew, Shiela, myself, Julie, Tim, Malcolm

CHAPTER NINE

COMING TO THE CROSS-ROADS

SNAFU photo-shoot at Richard Branson's Oxford studios 1971

During the lay-off period after SNAFU, one of my best friends at that time, Reg Isadore, would join me and we would have some crazy times together. I would meet many different musicians who offered me work but nothing seemed to be what I was looking for. Then I was approached by Joe Jammer, from Chicago and Tony Stevens, a bass player who had recently been with 'Fog Hat', who were big in America, and previously with 'Savoy Brown'. Joe and Tony were interesting because they had Julie Enthoven as their manager and it looked promising. She was the sister of David Enthoven, the Manager of Roxy Music and later

59

Robbie Williams. She introduced us to Max Clifford. Max believed we would be big and became very involved.

The new band they were forming at this time was called 'Nobody's Business' but before I could join the band one hundred per cent, there was an album I had to record for the late Tim Rose on the Côte d'Azur. Tim penned songs like 'Walk me out in the morning dew' and many more. How this brief episode came about was through the grapevine. I met John Bonham, who became the drummer for Led Zeppelin, and had been playing with Tim Rose. He asked me to stand in for him on the album for Tim.

So it was in the south of France that I met a French lady who was working in the market. Anyone 'different' interests me and she was a little unusual as she had a pet monkey. As soon as the monkey saw me it would shag my leg like it was another monkey it had not seen for ages – so embarrassing!

One evening, after a recording session, we had dinner and as we had accommodation at the studio, I ended up taking her back to my room. Of course the inevitable happened and we ended up in bed. To my astonishment she started to call out and I thought she wanted to go to the toilet but after a while I realised she was shouting "Yes", which of course in French, sounds like wee! It did distract me a little at the time, but not too much!

I had four weeks of wonderful wine, food and of course my little French fairy. After all this we did manage to get down the tracks in question.

On my return I had to pick up where I had left off with Max and Julie. We had Max Clifford as our publishing agent, and he and I became a very close and good friends.

We were very much alike in lots of ways, especially our love of football apart from everything else. I always knew Max would make it in some way or another because of his strong positive way. Take a look at where he is today. I believe he must have become a Christian type of person. We had wonderful times together and are still in touch.

'Nobody's Business' first engagement was to be in Ibiza, a two week trip that Max had organised for photographs to be taken. Also we played in the evenings at one of the major discos there. Here I met, needless to say another blond beauty called Pia, from Stockholm. Our relationship lasted for the entire trip.

An album simply called 'Nobody's Business' was recorded around this time but released only in Japan. On our return we had a meeting and I suggested we should lay down our first album at the studio I had previously been to on the Côte d'Azur in the south of France, where 'Pink Floyd' had by this time recorded 'Another brick in the wall'. I decided not to get involved with my little French fairy this time around and concentrate more on productive things. It took us about one month to record this album.

Now 'Nobody's Business' was booked to play in Chicago and although I felt it was not a good time to be leaving the family, as things were bad between Linda and I, I felt I had no choice and so I found myself in Chicago – with the worst weather ever recorded there! It was absolutely freezing and with the wind chill factor, temperatures reached minus forty but this was the least of my worries. Chicago was the sort of town which was full of hoods and gangsters. On one occasion I was on a bus going from the south to downtown when a man jumped on and snatched the nearest woman's handbag out of the blue and jumped off again. Everyone was shocked and hesitated in case he had a gun as muggings were always happening. This was 1976 and this kind of behaviour had yet to reach the UK.

Being a little vain I would have my trousers made especially for me with no pockets and they were taken in and made extra tight to show off my nice bum. Often women would make comments like "Lovely arse" and I would reply, "Doesn't say much for my face". These tight trousers meant I had to keep my money in my boots, which was probably the safest place to keep it anyway.

Whilst we were recording one day, there were a few friends of the band looking for a bit of smoke and cocaine between times of recording. A big American guy said he knew where we could score and did we want to go with him? I was one of the guys who happened to go along with him on this occasion. After we had been driving for about an hour we eventually came to a wooded area, like a small forest. We drove into the trees along a track for about ten minutes and came across a little camp of two or three log cabins. There were a few jeeps and cars parked around and after we had parked I followed my companion into one of the cabins. Inside there were a few men who appeared to be working and I noticed they were all wearing hip guns and shoulder holsters. I suddenly had this awful sinking feeling as I realised he had brought me to a drug den and these men were all dealers. I found this pretty scary and couldn't wait to get out of there. The police could turn up at anytime and there would have been a shoot out and who knows what may have happened from there. It took us about half an hour to get what we came for but it seemed like a life-time until we were on our way back to the studio.

It was on this tour, while waiting in a club called 'Mothers', that due to the length of time spent hanging around waiting to go on stage, I got really stoned. As I was bored, I spent the time drinking and taking what was going. Halfway through the act I nearly collapsed as it was too much for my system. This came as a big shock as I realised that I could have died. The next day was the turning point when I felt I had to give up drugs. It had frightened me so much, I knew I had to kick the habit before it killed me.

This was not going to be easy and to make matters worse, what I had been hoping would not happen was just about to. As I suspected the dreaded phone call came from Linda to say that I needn't bother about coming back. The locks had been changed and she had boxed up all my clothes and belongings and sent them to my agents. She said she was with someone else now. This was really bad news and on top of all that, as if that was not enough, I knew the man! He was the main dealer in cocaine around London at that time.

I was extremely concerned about the boys who were at a very young age and I felt helpless and sick with worry about them. Even though I knew I had been deceitful and unfaithful, I could not come to terms with the thought of this man bringing up my children.

At the end of the tour, I returned to the UK. I felt everything had gone pear-shaped and had fearful thoughts as I didn't know what awaited me on my return. I had to stay with my managers, Richard and Hermione and also with Julie Enthoven in London.

This was becoming the worst part of my life. I felt that I had lost everything and the guilt I felt was overwhelming. I felt I was reaping what I had sown. It was payback time. No wonder people murder their partners. I even had evil thoughts myself.

And yet, somewhere at the back of my mind I started to have Christian thoughts. Was someone trying to talk to me? I began to take a look at myself. I needed to sort myself out. At times I felt I would like to end it all, I was so low. I had hit rock bottom. I knew I had to move on. I knew that what had happened to me, although not fully realising at the time, was the most incredible loss, the biggest loss of all time. The only way out was up and I decided to change my life from the drugs and drink and knew I had to pull myself together.

Then another blow during this awful time came when Julie Enthoven died suddenly in a car crash in Chicago. Julie had been our manager along with Max and the members of 'Nobody's Business' were so affected by this tragic accident that we felt we could not carry on.

I went home to be with my parents for a while as this was the best place for me at this time. Although I did not get on with my father, I was very close with my mother and knew I was always loved with her around me.

So the journey was to take another course.

CHAPTER TEN

ICELAND

1983 arriving at Reykjavik, Iceland – new beginning

My mother was a great help and it was like starting all over again. As time passed, recovery came and I knew music would be my way forward. All this time I had kept in touch and knew of a band which was being formed and run by a couple of businessmen who did not know very much about the music scene.

At last here was another opportunity to form a band and so 'Niagara', was born, an all-black band, with me as the lead singer together with the Isadore brothers, Reg and

Gus. Reg, the drummer, had played with Robin Trower's band whilst Gus, his younger brother, played guitar. Later, Gus went on to play with Seal. They had an elder brother too, Conrad, who played with Joe Cocker and 'Crosby, Stills and Nash'.

Niagara's first test as a rock band was on the BBC with Tommy Vance. We made a recording of six tracks for the Tommy Vance show at the famous Abbey Road studios where the Beatles recorded many times. The outcome was Tommy on radio saying he "liked this band and they are going to go places".

It was during this time of recording that I met an old friend of mine, Anna. She was Icelandic, married to an English man who was a private detective and they lived in London. It was like jumping out of the frying pan into a massive furnace. I never do anything in small measures! I was on the rebound and as things turned out Anna became pregnant. She left her husband and returned home to Iceland to be with her family.

Ragnar, my son, was born there, a beautiful boy. Anna kept in touch with me and it was not long after that I decided to split from the band and join them both. It was a good reason to get away and make a fresh start, away from the drugs and music scene that I knew.

So on the 1st August 1980 I arrived at Keflavik Airport to be greeted by Anna and the hottest day on record in Iceland. On the final approach to Iceland it has such breathtaking scenery – if anyone has made this trip they will know what I am talking about. It can only be likened to landing on the moon. Little did I realise at the time what changes I was about to go through and, smack in the middle, I could feel the Lord step on board.

Something had happened. I was very excited about seeing my son for the first time and I felt it was the beginning of the Lord trying to reach me. The magic of the scenery also moved me so much I wrote one particular song, 'Looking for a Friend', about my desire to search for God, which I later recorded. I felt I was coming through, getting away from the drugs and my old self.

Anna worked at a hotel in Reykjavik, where she lived, and it was not long before I was working there, singing in the evenings. I was offered accommodation at the hotel as part of the deal and this worked out well as I did not want to put pressure on Anna but I could see my son Ragnar, who was now six months old, grow up.

The journey however was to take a new twist as, during my nights singing at the hotel, I met and fell in love with Margret and she was to eventually become my second wife.

I felt a wake up call in Iceland, the closest thing to God, with the nature of the place and the whole new life unfolding before me. It was early days but I could see and feel a potential in Iceland for promoting bands, which I eventually did. They had no blues bands and I was the first to perform as a blues artist.

After Margret and I were married, I felt it was the best thing that could have happened, and wanted to make a real go of things.

We both decided to leave Iceland and live in the UK and, to begin with, things went well, but gradually Margret became home-sick and missed her family.

At this time my brother had been involved in a bad accident and was in a coma for ten months before he died. This had a huge impact on the family, so after a while Margret and I decided to return to Iceland.

The preparations were in hand and to top it all I bought a car, not just any car, but a big white American Buick and we filled it up with goods. Margret booked a ferry which was to leave from Newcastle about eight in the morning so we set off early, before it was light. We were both looking forward to returning to Iceland especially with the new car. We arrived at Newcastle at about seven a.m. and found ourselves in a queue. It was just down to five cars in front of us when it was announced that the ship, a Polish ship, was full and the next one was not until the following Saturday, one week away.

The week was spent living on take-away food at a B&B in Newcastle – not a good start, but we made sure we were first in the queue next time and first on board the ship.

It took four days to reach Iceland, three of which I spent in bed with seasickness. It was a very rough crossing and I was so pleased to arrive and get back onto dry land again. The family was there to welcome us, as we had planned to stay with Margret's parents who owned a large guesthouse.

I got on well with Margret's parents, but I did have one problem and that was getting a job. There was the difficulty of the language and things were very expensive which didn't help either. Being a survivor though, and determined, I saw openings and bought myself a drum kit and soon I was working in some of the clubs. As a performer I started to make a name for myself and the next step was to sell the car.

This I did for double the price I had paid for it which gave me a nice feeling. I was very happy, and was straightening myself out now. I felt it had all come together for me. However, I was worried about my mother back in the UK especially as my brother had died and after a year had passed I decided to go and see her.

Margret was to stay behind this time as I did not intend to stay long but after arriving in England, I rang Margret and could not help noticing something was strange in her voice. I had experienced something like this in the past and I dreaded calling again as I was beginning to suspect something was wrong. I knew the signs. She was only twenty-one and I was in my early forties.

On return to Iceland the signs were all there, so I questioned her. The bad news came like a bolt through the heart. She had met someone else who she thought would give her better opportunities. I had to let her go and so we split. I stayed on at her parent's home and she moved in with her new man. I was devastated.

Margret's mother, Stefana, was a great help at this time and she felt sure that Margret would soon return home again. We became good friends during this time and sure enough, just as predicted, Margret came back after three months. It had been three months of wildness and confusion. Had this been my pay back time I wondered? I had been faithful and true. It had been a difficult time for me.

I decided we needed our own home so we moved out of Margret's parents' guesthouse into our own flat but, trust me, I chose a street name that was a real tongue twister!

It took me a whole month to learn how to pronounce it. In Icelandic it is spelt Braedraborgastigur – sounds like (Brave the bore gah steer gah).

We were both working and soon settled down to our new life together when one day, out of the blue, I received a letter from my daughter Louise. She had been living with her mother, Dorothy, in Canada and now she had reached the age of sixteen she had decided she would like to visit her father in Iceland. I was of course delighted and welcomed her with open arms but unfortunately the timing was not great, as Margret and I were just getting back together. I explained the situation to Louise and she agreed that she would stay with us for just two weeks.

Needless to say, Louise fell in love with Iceland and became adamant about staying on. This caused the situation to become uncomfortable so I explained that my marriage was not to suffer and she would have to look after herself. Well, she never looked back and to my amazement she not only learnt the language in three months but made a group of friends and also secured a job at the fish factory.

Louise is still living in Iceland today, in Selfoss, which is over the mountains from Reykjavik – the place where the tourists go to see the hot geysers and the glass houses where the vegetables are grown. She has done remarkably well on her own and now has a partner and three children, my grandchildren.

Soon after Louise arrived, Margret became pregnant and in due time our daughter Julia was born. I was there when she was born, on 16th August 1985 and found this one of the most amazing experiences of my life. I felt very moved and proud of her. It came as a big shock as I didn't realise just how painful giving birth can be and all that is involved. These were very happy days for me as I was enjoying being a father and life as a family felt extremely good.

CHAPTER ELEVEN

SOLID SILVER

My solo album 'Solid Silver' was recorded in Iceland featuring a group called 'Mezzoforte'. I found them rehearsing in a garage one day – they were only between eighteen and nineteen years old and they were magnificent.

During this period, knowing them, I helped their manager with some information about agents and record companies in London. Eventually they had their own top-twenty hit in the UK with the instrumental 'Garden Party'.

Gulli Briem was the drummer with Johann (Joey) Asmundsson on bass, Eythor Gunnarsson on keyboard and Fridrik Karlsson on guitar. Fridrik wrote some music for me on 'Solid Silver'.

Meanwhile, my good friend, Svanur, an ex-alcoholic, became a club owner and he asked me one night to perform as a solo act. I agreed to go along that night and do it for him. Little did I know what was in store for me that evening.

When I was taking a break at the bar, having a drink, suddenly I felt someone get hold of my long hair from behind me, pull me off the barstool and drag me along the dance floor. This was a shock and as I got up quickly to see what was happening, two American Air-force men, who must have been stationed at the local air base, had obviously had too much to drink and didn't like my image.

Before I knew it, one punched me on the nose and broke it in three places. Needless to say blood was everywhere. Unfortunately I was wearing a white top which was covered. Svanur, the owner, took me into the kitchen and patched me up. Then he sent me home in a taxi. It took two days for the bleeding to stop and then I was to attend the hospital who would straighten it out for me.

I wasn't sure how they would do this, as it was completely flat on my face, just like a boxer's. Margret came and watched as they attempted to straighten it out for me. The first thing they did was to stick three long needles about six inches long up each nostril and into the back of my face. This numbed the area and took about half an hour to take effect. I was then ushered into a small private room and told to sit down on a chair. The doctor was behind me and the usual remark came, "You won't feel a thing, but the cracking of the bone may make you feel sick".

With that remark, he put one arm around my neck and proceeded to crack my nose back into place. I can still hear it today, if I close my eyes. It took about a year to heal and quite sometime before I could breathe properly.

One of the original members in another group I formed, called 'Rockola', was called Billy Rock. He was unfortunately another alcoholic and then sadly, one day I heard he had died in a car crash whilst driving over the mountains in bad weather to play at a gig. He was only thirty-six years old. I was shocked to hear of his death.

CHAPTER TWELVE

SPLIT PROMO

As there were so few live bands in Iceland, Tony Sandy, who was a good friend at this time, got together with me and we decided to form a promotional company. The basis of this was to promote well-known bands to perform at the sports stadium, which held about five thousand people. We planned and promoted the likes of 'Meat Loaf', for two concerts, and 'Aha', 'Europe', 'Cock Robin' and 'Kiss'. This was very successful until we had two bands in succession, 'Status Quo' and 'Boy George', neither of which proved very successful with the Icelandic audience.

This was like gambling and the stakes were high. If we won, it was great, but if things were not so good, we could lose a lot of money. I wonder now if it was a substitute for the drugs as it was a dangerous game to play. In the end I was bankrupt. Then I received a telephone call from Tony who said he was calling from a ship on his way back to England. This was bad news as he owed me about ten thousand pounds – about half the bankruptcy money.

On top of all this Margret broke the news that she was going back to university for two years and was taking Julia with her – our marriage was over. Now I was alone in the home which gave me the feeling of being in a wilderness, not knowing what was around the corner. Should I stay in Iceland or leave? It was a big decision and I was at rock bottom again.

I am sure this was part of the Lords preparation. I was forced to sell our home and another journey was to begin. It was time to take a real good look at myself. I even heard a voice saying "Take a look at yourself". I was very down. I had lost my family again. I felt rejection, jealousy, isolation and loneliness.

I was still friendly with Margret's parents, but distant now and the weather didn't help, being in the middle of winter. I began to realise it had only been Julia keeping me there.

I decided to seek help and visited a church in Reykjavik and also went along to the A.A. centre. I was walking along one day and somehow the next minute I was inside, and found a group of people sitting around a table. They all seemed confused. They were people who had screwed up their lives and were searching, crying out for help. After half a dozen meetings I knew it was not for me. I was not an alcoholic, or a drug addict. I had already been there and done that. I was clean and past this.

I had put my money into bands, taking a chance, not acting responsibly for the family. When was I ever going to learn? I was always falling down and picking myself up again. Somehow I was paying for the past. I felt it was my pay back time from the Lord. I felt sure He had something more and then the voice came to say this time, "Go back to England".

So, I decided to return to England and as soon as I could, I set about selling the flat. Then I rang my friend, Pete Rogers, a drummer who lived in Braintree in Essex, a drummer who played jazz. Pete agreed to put me up for a while which was a great help. Another good friend, George

Fitzpatrick, a guitarist, mentioned some friends in London and after contacting them I secured a job to go back to. So another journey began on the 21st June 1991 when I arrived back in the UK.

After a couple of weeks, I thought about tracing Tony Sandy, as he still owed me some money. I remembered him mentioning Stroud, so I decided this was a good place to start my search. As I drove around the town centre I could not believe my luck. There was a hairdresser with exactly the same name and logo as Tony had used in Iceland. It was too much of a coincidence so, after parking the car, I walked in and came face to face with Tony.

I said, "You'd better ask you clients to leave" and then simply asked for my money back. After a few threats I managed to recover about half the money due to me although this was paid over a period of time as Tony paid it monthly. To this day I feel that the Lord led me on that day.

During the two weeks I stayed with Pete in Braintree, he mentioned that his niece, who had a place in Great Waltham, was looking for a tenant, so I went along to see if it would be suitable for me. It was just what I was looking for and I ended up staying there for three years. This was my stepping stone to the next chapter of my life.

CHAPTER THIRTEEN

THE TURNING POINT

Dave Cooke and myself – gigging

I was getting older now and feeling much more mature. I knew I could not mess up again this time and I could feel an inner closeness to the Lord.

I had become friends with Bev and Eddie, who were the publicans at the Beehive in Great Waltham. As I was living on my own at this time, I would have my meals there and they were always there to listen to a worldly tale of mine. I am glad to say we are still good friends today.

It was during this time I formed a duo with John Wilson. John played keyboard jazz and with me on the drums we were quite successful, especially in the Home Counties. Unfortunately John was another alcoholic. I tried to help him, but I knew it was really up to him and I thought in time, he would probably have to be replaced. Then came the day when John went missing and three gigs were lost. I knew I'd have to go and look for him.

John lived in Ilford and when I arrived, I knocked on the door but there was no answer. Not wanting to give up, I knocked again and again. Eventually there was a sound from inside and so I peered through the letter-box and saw John sliding down the stairs in his underwear, in a very sorry state.

He let me in, and as the door opened the smell hit me full on. The house stank of booze. John had collapsed two days ago and had been lying in his own vomit. He was lucky to be alive, as he could easily have choked on it and died.

I'd had some experience with alcoholics before, and decided I had to part with Mr Wilson. Also by now I believed someone was pointing the way and looking after me.

I already knew another keyboard player who was excellent and best of all he was a Christian, Dave Cooke. So a meeting was arranged with Dave and it was decided we would join forces. Dave's Christian faith was rubbing off on me now, big time. In the early days he was a role model and taught me a great deal from all his experiences.

Of course we had our ups and downs. Dave was trying to make me see the truth about what was going on in my life and what I should do about it. I felt sure the Lord had placed us together and the Lord was beginning to work on my case.

While we were playing together at gigs I had to deal with women again. There was one special lady I liked and I enjoyed her company. Her name was Doreen and we seemed to have everything going for us, except I was beginning to have faith now and I felt I was doing the wrong thing. I just felt it was not right, like I was taking advantage of her and I felt guilty about this. Unfortunately Doreen became ill and was then diagnosed with breast cancer. She died just a few short months later, leaving me feeling very distraught and helpless. It was an extremely sad time.

Sometime afterwards I was giving an interview on the BreezeFM radio station with Romilly Paradine. She and I met afterwards for a drink and hit it off immediately, spending the next six years together!

During this time I felt the Lord was becoming stronger and stronger within me, and taking more control over my life. I knew I could not mess around with the Lord and I had to choose. I knew the Lord was the way forward, which meant living by the truth. It frightened the life out of me at the time and I wondered if I could. I had always ducked and dived through life and camouflaged the truth. I knew I had to give up everything. Everything that was bad, like living with someone and not marrying them, or evading the tax man. I had a choice – I could stay as I was and keep messing up, but to keep messing up made me unhappy.

I was beginning to learn, "You reap what you sow", but I needed help. So the decision became easy now as I knew I wanted the Lord in my life.

Of course, once this decision is made, the devil comes into play as he does not want to lose you, and consequently a war was starting to brew, a spiritual war.

On one of my trips into Southend, I found myself walking into a Christian Fellowship meeting, which was held there. It was similar to my experience in Iceland when I had just walked into the AA meeting. This time I was on the stairs when I met someone called Mark Churchward who invited me in and spoke with me for sometime. This had a great impact on me and I attended more meetings and discussions on a weekly basis. This was preparing me for the time to become a Christian, therefore I had to confess all my sins.

I had been thinking for some time that living with Romilly was not right in the Lord's eyes. Then I was invited to move in with some Christian friends until I could get my own flat and I knew this was the right way forward. I also knew this was going to be painful for both of us.

This was my first real move on the Christian journey. There were weeks of Bible studies and long talks before finally, I was baptised and I was able to start a relationship properly with the Lord. My baptism was a very special day for me, and my 'prophecies' are included at the end of this book. Please take the time to read them.

Now I had a flat of my own and was beginning to give up things, which I found very difficult. On top of this I was lonely. I knew I had to carry on and go through this. Looking back I now know this was 'the wilderness'. It was so difficult to deal with the devil and I felt all sorts of things were happening to me.

Around this time and whilst playing at a gig, I met Lisa, whom I had known from the past, way back in the early days. I fell hopelessly in love with her yet at the same time I knew it was the devil's work. Women were my biggest weakness!

Lisa was very attractive. She was half Indian with two children and even though I knew it was the devil's work I still succumbed to his temptation – even though I knew it would be another woman hurt and I would end up hurt too. I knew I had to tell her that it was not going to work. She was not a Christian and I had to choose. It was war going on between the devil, Lisa, myself, and the Lord – and the Lord won. I chose the Lord.

Now I knew I had to face the aftermath. I felt anxious, as if I was losing things slightly.

Then I applied for a private hire driving job, which was offered to me and that lifted my spirits. It would mean a two-month wait, which was not so good as I really needed something to take my mind off things, but I still had to face more time in the wilderness.

I was only a baby as far as Christianity was concerned so when an old friend suggested I should see a medium, I made a big mistake and went to visit one. I now feel this too was the devil's work. I just wanted to get Lisa out of my mind but I was going against the Lord in seeing a medium.

After my visit, I became very ill and my doctor had to prescribe anti-depressants. It would appear that the medium had put me into a trance and I was still there. It was some time before I came out of it.

It was a gradual recovery and when I felt better and had time to reflect, I realised it was the work of the Lord flushing out all the old poison in my body, sweating it out, all the bad stuff in my life.

CHAPTER FOURTEEN

NEW LIFE

My Young Friends

The new job was just what I needed, a new beginning. Now I could see the light at the end of the tunnel.

The new job involved driving special-needs children to their school everyday and home again. Also, I was still playing music with Dave Cooke and we were a successful duo at this time.

Out of this came another offer, a Christian job. A friend, Graham Bannister, needed help with a project the church were organising. I knew it was a tough one but I also knew that it was part of my Christian training. The project was a brilliant idea called 'Bar'n'Bus' and was for children who were on the streets, had nowhere to go and whose parents didn't really care about them or what they were doing. Most were on wiz, speed or sniffing glue.

An old London bus was used and parked in the Asda car park at Shoeburyness. Downstairs the bus had been converted into a café serving tea and cakes. Upstairs was used as a place to chat and help and advice was available if needed. Some of the kids were so lovely, they gave me a great buzz and I looked forward to this project in the evenings.

There were a few incidents, and on one particular occasion a young boy was stabbed in the head. Fortunately, and thankfully, he made a good recovery. There were approximately six staff including Sue Norris, who became a close friend, plus the driver.

Also this is where I met a young Christian lady called Wendy Mitchell who came to help one night. Wendy would sometimes bring her daughter, Charlotte along and we became good friends and the relationship grew and eventually led to us getting married. We are still together today living in Southend with Charlotte of course.

It is so nice to feel the support of Wendy and Charlotte. I like to encourage Charlotte who is twelve years old, with her dancing and singing which she performs most evenings for me. It is wonderful entertainment, better than watching Madonna or Britney Spears.

At this time I was based at Shoeburyness and Thorpe Bay Baptist church and I decided to form a band within the church called 'Journey'. The members of the band are all Christians and we play for charity at gigs all over Essex and other places to raise money for the likes of Cancer Research, Leprosy and many more. The band is still playing today and hopefully has saved a few souls as well as raising money.

Just as I thought everything was now hunky-dory, I heard the voice again. This time it was to remind me that there was one other matter to be dealt with from my past, the dreaded tax man. I knew I couldn't hide from this anymore. I decided to put my hands up and inform the Inland Revenue and face the music but I also prayed to the Lord to help me through this. It took a total of three years to reach a settlement and you can imagine how frightening at the time this felt. I prayed every day, nearly all day.

I did feel the Lord was helping me through this time of worry but I had bad dreams about the lady who was dealing with my case. Her name was Mrs Dougal. She would appear in my dream waving a big stick at me, giving me nightmares. The whole tax experience had been a nightmare giving me three years of paranoia and when it was all over I felt the sense of the most incredible freedom which I had never experienced before. At this point I would like to thank Roger Barnard, my accountant and guitarist in 'Journey', for his patience and help through those three years.

The time seemed right now for my autobiography. I remembered what Graham Bannister had said on the 'Bar'n'Bus' – "You should take time out to write a book". I also had my comrades and brothers telling me to get on with this project as I had been talking about it for some time!

But I needed to feel clean. I could not really become a witness to anyone if I hadn't cleaned my act up. How could I give advice knowing I hadn't paid my £40,000 taxes? It would have been hypocritical. Now is the right time.

Procul Harum star Bobby books in

IN PRINT: Bobby Harrison with his new autobiography Journey to Freedom.

Picture by Martin Dalton

By Karen Davis

A MEMBER of chart-topping 60s band Procul Harum hopes the publication of his autobiography will inspire people to pick up an instrument.

Bobby Harrison, who splits his time between his families in Southend and Iceland, said writing the book was like therapy for him.

He said: "It was hard reliving some of the painful memories but I wanted to be as truthful as possible without hurting anyone.

"All of me is in the book, and I think it will be a great read as well as a cautionary tale."

As well as inspiring new muscians, Bobby hopes it will warn people about the pitfalls of drugs and alcohol.

Bobby came to Southend in 1966 when he joined Procul Harum. The band's song, A Whiter Shade of Pale, is one of the biggest selling records of all time.

He has since released several solo albums and worked with groups such as Mezzoforte.

Bobby's next concert is at the Plaza Centre, in Southchurch Road, Southend, on Tuesday, September 16, with his latest band, Journey and Friends.

His autobiography - entitled Journey to Freedom - will be published on October 25.

For more information visit journey2freedom.co.uk

WUFF JUSTICE: Sergeant Neil Phimister with Wills and Boots.   Picture by Martin Dalton

Police dog unit opens its doors

By Matthew Stanton

THE HISTORY of dogs at Essex Police is about be showcased.

Residents have been invited to the Essex Police Dog Unit Open Day, in Sandon, on Saturday, August 30.

A free park and ride from Sandon School, in Molrams Lane, will take people to the event, which starts at 11am.

Inspector Martin Parkin said: "This Open Day is a unique opportunity for people to look around the section and see the dogs demonstrate their skills.

"The dog unit is vital in helping to keep Essex safe. We are very proud of them and want to show their skills to the community."

Essex Police Dog Unit currently has 45 German Shepherds, one Malinois, 12 Springer Spaniels and four Labradors.

CHAPTER FIFTEEN

A WHITER SHADE OF PALE

14 NEWS   THE TIMES WEDNESDAY NOVEMBER 15 2006

I turned pale effort into a cult classic, says organist

By Lucy Bannerman

A FORMER drummer from Procol Harum told the High Court yesterday of the 'before' and 'after' versions of A Whiter Shade of Pale in which it was transformed from an unknown demo into a world-wide hit.

Robert Harrison, 67, who had been with the band at its peak, spoke of how the original material sounded significantly different after the addition of the Hammond organ.

The song, released in 1967, is the subject of a legal battle between Gary Brooker, the vocalist and co-writer, and Matthew Fisher, a computer programmer, who claims that he deserves an authorship credit for providing the single's organ instrumental.

Mr Harrison was himself engaged in a legal battle with Mr Brooker for royalty rights before a confidential settlement in 1969. Yesterday in court he recalled visiting Mr Brooker in 1967, when the musician played him material recorded before Mr Fisher's arrival. Mr Harrison said: "There was bass, drums and piano, but I don't remember a Hammond. I think it is significant because it didn't have the organ on it." When he heard the song later at his audition, it had been transformed by the organ. "That's when I heard the difference," he said.

Mr Brooker and Keith Reid, who share the authorship rights, approached Mr Fisher, an organist, because they believed the Hammond would give them a unique sound.

Mr Harrison saw the vocalist as the leader of Procol Harum, but the organ player as a key member, the court was told. "I was always under the impression that Matthew was one of the main writers of the band."

Earlier, Mr Fisher told the court that he felt aggrieved not only because of alleged unpaid royalties, estimated at £1 million but also because he had lost his place in British musical history. He said: "It was not until the mid-1980s that the song began to acquire its cult classic status. Here we have a song which is going to go down in history which ought to have my name on it, and it doesn't."

Asked under cross-examination whether he made the claim only after nearly four decades of reaping the benefits as a member of Procol Harum, Mr Fisher replied: "That's the funniest thing I've heard. If I could go back in time, I would not have joined Procol Harum. I would have joined another band."

When Andrew Sutcliffe, QC, representing Mr Brooker, put it to Mr Fisher that when the song was first presented at rehearsal,

'It is a fiction that he wrote this tune and I just adapted it. That is completely false'

it was complete, and featured the distinctive Bach-inspired introduction, he replied: "The writing Keith and Gary were doing needed fleshing up. I reject any suggestion that there was any memorable tune."

Mr Fisher did not deny that it had been Mr Brooker's original idea to compose a song based on Bach's compositions Air on a G-String and Sleepers Awake. He said: "I thought that was brilliant, but he didn't really have the background to carry it through to its conclusion. I came in to finish the job.

"If you take out my contributions, you would have had a song that would never have been released. We're getting into this fiction that he wrote this tune and I just adapted it. That is completely false."

The hearing continues.

Gary Brooker co-wrote the song, but Matthew Fisher, right, claims that he deserved a credit

Procol Harum royalty battle

It was during the writing of this book that, out of the blue one evening, I received a phone call from my old friend, Matthew Fisher, from 'Procol Harum'.

It sounded like he'd had a couple of drinks, just a little wobble in his voice here and there, but I did get the gist of the conversation which was that he wanted to sue Gary Brooker for royalties on a 'A Whiter Shade of Pale'.

My reply was, "Don't you think it's a bit late?"

"My lawyers do not think so," he replied. "It is not the money I am after, but the going down in history for such an iconic song, which I was definitely a part of."

With a deep breath on the other end of the phone, "Will you be my witness?"

I replied, "Give me a couple of days to think about it". Matthew did call me back after a couple of days and I had thought about it and decided to go ahead with Matthew, because I knew the truth, he was a co-writer. I had in my past career, like so many others, been ripped off and I just felt this was terribly wrong. Gary Brooker was a millionaire and Matthew Fisher was struggling.

So a little time went by and then in the post came the date of the case which was to be held in the Royal High Court of Justice in the Strand in London in December 2006. I was feeling a little nervous, obviously, about seeing the old faces after so long but it could also be a wonderful experience to see them again.

I had previously prepared my statement which I had signed and sent off. A couple of days later I thought the Lord was trying to remind me of something and I suddenly remembered I had omitted something very significant to the case. I had heard the song 'A Whiter Shade of Pale' for the first time at Gary's house in 1967, when I was invited there to prepare for my audition for 'Procol Harum' – *without the organ music on it.*

On the day of my audition, I heard the song again with the organ being played on it this time. It seemed to be a whole different sound with much more colour and if you know this song, which I am sure most of you do, you will know this is the selling point, along with the voice of course and the overall feeling.

This was a very significant part of my statement that had come into my head after signing and submitting it. Now though, it was too late to amend it.

When we arrived at the High Court it was so grand, it was a real historic English building with over fifty courts. Unfortunately we were in Court 56 which I was not happy about as it meant quite of lot of walking to do – I had a dodgy knee, with a worn-out cartilage.

Pete and David, my two Christian friends, had come with me so we made our way together across the marble stone floors busy with people dressed in black robes and wearing wigs. The atmosphere was amazing.

On arrival at Court 56 we were ushered in and had to bow to the Judge before taking our seats. It was a dark panelled courtroom and the Judge was wearing a black robe with a red sash and a wig.

The next thing was a very natural thing to do and that was to look around and see who I could recognise, bearing in mind we were all forty years older. I saw Matthew right away as he was in the witness box and then I spotted Gary sitting with his lawyers looking very bored. I also saw Gary's wife Frankie, Keith Reid was next and he was looking ultra miserable. I spotted many other famous faces too.

This, to me, brought a sense of sadness and loss, because I remembered all the great times and fun and joy we had had touring around the world in the sixties and there we were now, a bunch of grumpy old men. This hurt me but of course this is life.

So I listened for an hour or two to Matthew's statements which were all very interesting as I found out lots of things which I never knew. I also found out I had played on ninety percent of the first album, which had 'gone platinum'.

The daylight was fading and I thought I might have to stay in London for the night. Then suddenly, I was called to the witness stand and I did all the usual things with my hand on the Bible and settled down. Gary Brooker's lawyer approached me and from out of the blue, would you believe it, the very first question he put to me was, "Were you at Gary Brooker's house in 1967 listening to "A Whiter Shade of Pale" in its original state, without the organ?"

I thought to myself, the Lord is here. This is the significant part that I had left out of my statement and was anxious to put right. I had been worried that I would never be able to add this important piece of information to my part of the evidence and now it was being asked of me, right at the onset, the very first question for me to answer.

I jumped in and said, "Yes, the first time I heard it, there was no organ music on it". I then went on to explain "The next time I heard it was at my audition – this time with the organ on it, which Matthew had played". I also said how much more colourful the song had sounded and it was a significant selling point of the song.

After more cross-examination, I could see Gary Brooker was getting more upset but Matthew Fisher had a slight grin on his face. I thought to myself I won't be on Gary's Christmas list in future.

So, my statement was over and we were allowed to go home. On the way home I felt very unhappy about the whole experience. It was the end of an era. I had helped a friend from the past but also lost a good friend from the past. I suppose it worked out equal for me with my conscience but I was glad it was over.

Unfortunately the media made a complete meal of it all, like they do, another bruise for the song which had bruised us all, but on reflection "A Whiter Shade of Pale" and 'Procol Harum' have been a very great part of, and a great help in my life.

A report of the court case by Jill Lawless, Associated Press writer, dated Monday 13th November 2006:

LONDON (AP) Two former 1960s rock stars appeared before a music-loving judge on Monday for a showdown over authorship of one of the decade's most iconic songs.

The organ strains of Procol Harum's 'A Whiter Shade of Pale' sounded through Court 56 of Britain's High Court as the band's former organ player, Matthew Fisher, sued an ex-band mate for a share of copyright in the multi-million selling song. Fisher's lawyer, Ian Purvis, said, "The song defined what is sometimes called the summer of love in 1967" and had achieved cult status. He said Fisher had composed the organ melody, and particularly the eight-bar Hammond organ solo which gives the song its distinctive baroque flavour.

Purvis said "The solo is a brilliant piece of work and it is crucial to the success of the song. Our case, in essence, is that Mr Fisher wrote the entirety of the organ tune." He said "Fisher is suing Procol Harum singer Gary Brooker and publisher Onward Music Ltd. for a co-author credit and a share of the songs copyright and royalties".

Brooker, who is credited as the song's author with lyricist Keith Reid, says the pair wrote the song before Fisher joined the band in March 1967.

Brooker has said the melody was inspired by Johann Sebastian Bach's "Air on a G String", and "Sleepers Awake."

Defence lawyers said the fact Fisher had waited almost four decades to bring his claim was "bizarre and obviously prejudicial. Mr Fisher's claim should fail on that ground alone" they said in court papers.

The song, renowned for its mystifying lyrics beginning "We skipped the light fandango, turned cartwheels cross the floor" topped the British singles chart for five weeks and was a top 10 hit in the United States. Rolling Stone magazine has ranked it 57th in a list of the 500 greatest songs of all time.

Purvis said a Web site compiled by a fan, lists 771 recorded cover versions, "most of them, sad to say, disastrous."

Fisher, now a computer programmer, left the band in 1969. Brooker, 61, still tours with 'Procol Harum'. The two sat facing Judge William Blackburne and did not look at one another on the first day of the five-day hearing.

Judge Blackburne later asked Fisher to play the organ melody on an electronic keyboard near the witness box.

Judge Blackburne, who studied both music and law at Cambridge University, requested access to the keyboard and sheet music of "A Whiter Shade of Pale" so he could run through the song after court hours.

Judges are not always familiar with popular music, and Purvis noted that "one always risks, in these cases a, 'what-are-The-Beatles?' moment", a reference to a famous but possibly apocryphal story of a judge who purportedly asked that question during a case in the 1960s.

"But I'll hazard a guess that your lordship is familiar with 'A Whiter Shade of Pale'," Purvis said.

"I am of an age, yes," said the 62-year old judge.

As I write this book, the court case is still going on.

APPENDIX ONE

FREEDOM

From James McCarraher's book 'Angel Air'

"Another gem from Angel Air Records sees these two albums get a long overdue re-release. 'Through The Years' should have set them up as major competition for 'Led Zeppelin'. Excellent informative cover notes as always help make this a stunning release."

Terry Craven, Wondrous Stories (May 1999)

The Freedom, (as they were then known) were formed in 1967 following a well publicised split within the ranks of Procol Harum.

Ray Royer (guitar) and Bobby Harrison (drums) founded the band which offered Bobby the creative freedom to flourish as a musician, songwriter and bandleader. It is fair to say that had he remained with Procol Harum, he may not have achieved his full potential.

Ray and Bobby recruited Mike Lease on keyboards and Steve Shirley on bass, thereby completing the line-up.

The band recorded their debut album, a soundtrack for the Italian film Nerosubianco, (Black on White). Disappointingly, it only received limited release in Italy, much to the frustration of all concerned.

Indeed, Bobby was very unhappy with the way matters were progressing and took the decision to dismiss the band and start again.

Simplifying the name to Freedom, he recruited Roger Saunders and Walter Monaghan. Freedom became a power trio much in the vein of Cream and The Jimi Hendrix Experience, churning out high quality heavy blues-rock.

In 1968, the album 'Freedom At Last', was unleashed upon the French and German record buying public but for some inexplicable reason did not receive a UK release. This was again a source of frustration for Bobby.

Nevertheless, the band worked hard and toured relentlessly, including trips to America supporting Jethro Tull and Black Sabbath. Slowly but surely, they built up a following and gained a formidable reputation as a live act.

The two following albums, 'Freedom' (1970) and 'Through The Years' (1971), received releases in both the UK and America, which meant that the band were at last reaching a greater audience.

Around the time of the release of the final album, 'Is More Than a Word' (1972), the future of Freedom looked bleak. Roger Saunders had secured a solo deal and the management sacked Walter Monaghan.

Two new members were introduced (Pete Dennis on bass and Steve Jolly on guitar) but Freedom had started drifting towards a sound more generally associated with Procol Harum.

In 1972, disillusioned and disappointed, the band split up.

The whole Freedom back catalogue has now deservedly been re-released on compact disc by Angel Air.

In the 21st Century, Bobby Harrison occasionally takes a version of Freedom on the road as a Christian rock band.

Reviews for *'Freedom at Last'* SJOCD175

"This is music from the late Sixties that is influenced by bands such as Cream. For me this is one of the most-played releases that I have had from Angel Air, as it is such an easy album to get into, yet there are so many layers that each time I play it I get even more from it. Plenty of information in the booklet makes this a wonderful release."

Feedback (September 2004)

"...a quality album. An amazing power trio, this is probably the missing link between sixties bands like Cream and the Jimi Hendrix Experience, and more experimental outfits like Led Zep', Deep Purple and the harder edge that The Who developed. A great gem of an album, released with impeccable presentation that sets every Angel Air release apart from the crowd."

Classic Rock Society (September 2004)

Reviews for *'Freedom'* SJPCD063

"By the time Procol Harum spin-off group Freedom recorded this eponymous album, they'd long since abandoned that group's classical roots in favour of a coarser, Cream/Sabbath-style progressive blues template. The presence of three would-be lead singers helped Freedom to wring the max from the formula. They were probably cracking live."

Classic Rock (August 2000)

"This delightful period piece is redolent of The Who circa Live at Leeds. The sleeve notes also contain a brilliant anecdote about Ozzy Osbourne flinging excreta at Curved Air's Sonja Kristina.

John Hazlewood, Q (August 2000)

Reviews for *'Through the Years'* SJPCD177

"They mix the blues in with more straightforward hard rock...another interesting nugget from Angel Air and one that is worth hearing.

Feedback (November 2004)

"Listeners will be transported to head-banging heaven.

Trevor Hodgett, Blues in Britain, (November 2004)

Reviews for *'Is More Than a Word'* SJPCD073

"The fact that the original LP is rated at £100 is more than welcome for fans. Mixing blues-rock, funk, and gentle piano-based seventies pop, the atmosphere is very upbeat. Although sadly, Freedom never made the first division of British rock this quality package is well worth checking out.

Joe Geesin, Record Collector (February 2001)

"A triumph of heavy blues rock and psychedelic pop which brought favourable comparisons with the likes of Cream and Led Zeppelin, and justifiably so. By the time of this release, Freedom had abandoned their hard blues driven approach for a funkier, more soulful sound.

Steve Ward, Wondrous Stories (February 2001)

APPENDIX TWO

BOBBY HARRISON

From James McCarraher's book 'Angel Air'

"For me, Harrison stands for part of my musical past and this album has enough to intrigue me."

Adrian Lyth, Classic Rock Society

We have already met Bobby Harrison through his band Freedom. Between 1968 and 1972, they produced a handful of superb albums, all of which have been re-released by Angel Air.

When Freedom disbanded, Bobby chose to pursue a solo career. Pulling together some of the biggest names in the business, he recorded a funk-driven album, appropriately named 'Funkist'. The recordings featured Herbie Flowers, Clem Cattini (ex-Johnny Kidd) Tony Iommi, Ray Owen and Micky Moody, to name but a few.

The album was released by Capitol Records in America and peaked at number 76 on the Billboard chart. Despite selling tens of thousands of units, Bobby failed to see a dollar in royalties. The album was never released in the UK

'Funkist' served as a bridge between Bobby's old band, Freedom and his new project, SNAFU.

Bobby founded SNAFU with old friend Micky Moody. They recruited Terry Popple on drums (ex-Tramline), and Colin Gibson (ex-Ginger Baker's Air Force) on bass. The line up was completed by keyboard wizard and fiddle player, Pete Solley. So began one of the finest and most soulful British acts of the mid-seventies.

The chemistry between the five musicians was very special and they ploughed a creative but uncommercial furrow, much in the vein of Little Feat and The Allman Brothers.

They recorded three albums before disbanding. All three have been re-released by Angel Air and are featured later in this book.

Following the break up of SNAFU, Bobby relocated to Chicago where he spent a couple of years gigging.

Whilst in America, he met an Icelandic lady and settled with her in Reykjavik, opting for a quieter life away from the rush and chaos of the Windy City.

He recorded an album in the mid-Eighties with Icelandic jazzers Mezzoforte, with a view to promoting himself in his new homeland:-

"It was all done very basically, very 'first take etc' I think we recorded the whole of that album in three days flat. It was done at a really good studio in Reykjavik though, called Steema."

The end result was called 'Solid Silver' which has now been re-released by Angel Air, complementing and concluding the Bobby Harrison career retrospective. This is the first time the album has been made available outside of Iceland.

Bobby had a hankering for his roots and returned to his native Southend. He now leads a quiet life as a committed born-again Christian.

Reviews for *'Funkist'* SJPCD056

"... a first-time-on-CD reissue for what many fans consider the missing link between his careers with Freedom and SNAFU. Funkist featured contributions from fellow future SNAFU man Micky Moody, Humble Pie's Clem Cattini, Deep Purple's Ian Paice, Black Sabbath's Tony Iommi, Procol Harum's Matthew Fisher, Wings' Henry McCulloch and Juicy Lucy's Ray Owen.

Jo-Ann Greene, Goldmine (April 2000)

"...there is plenty of funk and soul mixed with the blues-based rock that Bobby is best known for. The whole album is an easy mix, and Purple or Sabbath fans shouldn't expect too much heaviness. It's a real gem, nonetheless.

Record Collector (June 2000)

Reviews for *'Solid Silver'* SJPCD011

"It's always pleasing to get something from a musician that you remember from the 70's but you wondered what he was doing now. The original drummer with Procol Harum, founding member of Freedom, and lead singer with Seventies rockers SNAFU, Bobby Harrison has a pedigree. This album is a step in another direction, a lot more blues and AOR but the aforementioned pedigree shines through.

It's one of those albums where Harrison's voice is supported by neat jazz saxophone and piano solos and is always upbeat except where Harrison sings a purposeful ballad like the opener 'It's Over' or if he gets ultra bluesy as on 'Hot Stuff'. Second track, 'The Hunter', has opening bars that reminded me so much of 'Spirit in the sky' while the sax is covered superbly on 'Overload' by Stefan Stefanson.

For me Harrison stands for part of my musical past and this album has enough to intrigue me.

Adrian Lyth, Classic Rock Society

"The album features many differing musical styles, from big, clenched fist AOR ballads to blues rock. Mezzaforte's influence on the sound is immense and the jazzy saxophone and luscious electric piano chords are an unusual but effective accompaniment to Harrison's blues soaked delivery ... by and large this is an enjoyable album of jazz tinged blues rock.

Steve Ward, Wondrous Stories (Feb 2002)

'Angel Air – Where the Artist Has a Voice'
Isbn No 978-0-9526690-2-9
available direct from the Angel Air website
www.angelair.co.uk

APPENDIX THREE

SNAFU

From James McCarraher's book 'Angel Air'

"... you'll find appearances are deceptive; the laidback country-rock groove sustained throughout has held up remarkably well in the quarter-century since its release. Had it come from an American band, 'All Funked Up' would undoubtedly have done better"

Michael Heatley, Classic Rock (April 2000)

'SNAFU' is an acronym for 'Situation Normal, All Fucked Up' It is a phrase that was adopted by the military during either the First or Second World War (probably the latter) and was used by the Americans in Vietnam. The phrase is used to describe a confused or perilous situation.

SNAFU could be described as an early super group, pulled together from the crème de la crème of musicians around during the mid seventies.

The band was founded by Bobby Harrison (featured earlier in this book). Bobby had just left the group Freedom and embarked upon a solo album with the help of ex-Juicy Lucy front man Micky Moody. Such was the success of the collaboration that they decided to form a band with an R and B/funk slant.

Bobby and Micky recruited drummer Terry Popple, (ex-Tramline), bass player Colin Gibson (ex-Ginger Baker's Air Force) and keyboard wizard and fiddle player, Pete Solley.

So began the career of one of the funkiest, finest and most soulful British acts of the era.

The chemistry between the musicians was very special and they ploughed a creative but un-commercial furrow, much in the vein of Little Feat and The Allman Brothers.

They recorded their debut album, "SNAFU", at Richard Branson's Manor Studio and took their show on the road, supporting The Doobie Brothers in Europe and The Eagles in America. They were adored by audiences and critics alike.

The band reconvened for a second album, 'Situation Normal'. They knew that touring was the key to their success and were paired up with Emerson Lake and Palmer for an American tour. It was a mismatch and did not further their cause.

SNAFU's third and final album, 'All Funked Up', was recorded without Pete Solley who left to join Procol Harum (a band which had previously featured Bobby Harrison). Solley was replaced by Brian Chatton (and later by Tim Hinkley).

Sadly this line-up was short lived and Micky Moody left to join David Coverdale. SNAFU had run its course and disbanded.

Angel Air has paired the first two albums as a double CD release. The release of 'All Funked Up' is the first time the album has been made available in this format.

Review of 'Situation Normal'. SJPCD030

"This double album features two albums recorded by the band in the early seventies. I can remember catching the band at Reading Festival and with a line-up including Micky Moody on guitar and Bobby Harrison on vocals and a sound similar to Lynyrd Skynyrd, success seemed just around the corner. However, all the members of SNAFU moved on eventually to bigger things and SNAFU were just another part of Rock'n'Roll history. Maybe, but they were one of only a couple of bands from the U.K. to challenge that southern States style – and sound convincing. Moody's use of mandolin on SNAFU enhanced the idea of such a UK-based band challenging the mighty Americans and on 'Monday Morning' they achieved just that. Hearing Moody and SNAFU play in this style would convince even the biggest non-believer that rock was really great fun in the seventies.

'Situation Normal' is my favourite, with The Allman Brothers and Little Feat becoming heavier influences, those being favourite bands of Harrison. The debut album was actually recorded at the famous Manor at the same time as Tubular Bells and (Pete) Solley actually plays on that album briefly. Meanwhile, the band toured with the Doobie Brothers and The Eagles; no surprise there, as that was their stage. Solley's control and country influence becomes more apparent the more you listen to 'Situation Normal' and as the sleeve notes say, 'It makes you either love it or hate it'. Songs like 'Brown Eyed Beauty' and 'The Blue Assed Fly' helped me to love it.

The hit single though never came and they had to support ELP in the States which turned out to be a total mistake; they simply weren't that sort of band. By the third album, again recorded at the Manor, Solley was missing and for several reasons the band diminished which was a damned shame. Harrison has attempted to form SNAFU more recently but found it impossible as the original band was a unique combination. Never mind, there's always these greats.

Martin Hudson, Classic Rock Society

Review of *'All Funked Up'*. SJPCD032

"All Funked Up is SNAFU's elusive third album re-issued on CD for the first time. The blues debt is evident... while the Billy Gibbons-like overdriven slide adds a touch of Southern boogie to the mixture.

Joel McIver, Record Collector (April 2000)

'Angel Air – Where the Artist Has a Voice'
Isbn No 978-0-9526690-2-9
available direct from the Angel Air website
www.angelair.co.uk

APPENDIX FOUR

BAPTISM PROPHESIES

For Bobby Harrison at your baptism 22nd March 1998

Mark Churchward – "Bobby, I just wanted to share these two things – when I was preparing for this morning I felt I'd just like to kick off by praying for you and then anybody else join in as you want to. There are two scriptures – one from Jeremiah and one from Ephesians. "For I know the plans I have for you" declares the Lord. "plans to prosper you and not to harm you, plans to give you hope and a future." (Jeremiah 29:11)

Then, from Ephesians, I really feel this is for you this morning Bobby. "I pray also, (this is Paul writing, but, this is also our prayer for you). I pray also that the eyes of your heart may be enlightened in order that you may know the hope to which he has called you, the riches of his glorious inheritance in the saints (that's us) and his incomparably great power for us who believe." (Ephesians 1:18-19)

And Lord, as we're before you this morning, I want to pray that that will be Bobby's inheritance, that he will see those plans that you've prepared, those things that you've called him for, unfold clearly, and I want to pray Lord that he will know the hope that is in you, that in his heart there will be a rising of that hope that is born of knowing you, that he will know the riches of his inheritance in you Lord. This is a talented man in the natural but we pray Lord that you will pour into him the riches of his personal inheritance in Jesus, those things Lord that you've already prepared for him to enjoy, those things that you're going to release into his life that are part of his unique inheritance in you, and we pray Lord that he will know that incredible power with which you raised Jesus from the dead, at work in his life, that he will know your power, that he will know your touch, he will know your hand transforming him, transforming his circumstances, leading him in what you've prepared for him. Holy Spirit, we ask you to come today as Bobby stands before us, witnesses of his confidence and trust in Jesus. Holy Spirit we ask you to come to seal in his heart this covenant, this agreement, this mutual commitment, you to him and him to you, and that your power will rest upon him.

Pat Ransom – I believe God is saying this to you, "Bobby my son, keep my words and store up my commands within you. Keep my commands and you will live. Guard my teachings as the apple of your eye. Bind them on your fingers. Write them on the tablet of your heart. Say to wisdom "You are my sister," and call understanding your kinsman". (Proverbs 7:1-4)

And wisdom says this "I love those who love me and those who seek me find me. With me are riches and honour, enduring wealth and prosperity. My fruit is better than fine gold. What I yield surpasses choice silver. I walk in the way of righteousness along the paths of justice, bestowing wealth on those who love me and making their treasuries full". (Proverbs 8:17-21)

When I was thinking about you earlier, I just saw written all over you, "Wisdom", that God is going to fill you with wisdom. He's going to fill you. It's not just going to be written through you like a stick of rock, but it's going to over flow and others will come to hear God's wisdom through you.

Colin Geach – I believe God is saying "Bobby my son, I want you to know that I'm going to make you whiter than white. I'm going to make you a whiter shade of white because I am your righteousness. I am your righteousness and as you've proved the depths and the difficulties of life and so I'm going to prove to you the depths of my righteousness and the breadth of my righteousness and the height of my righteousness and you're going to prove that I am a righteous God and I'm going to reach you to reach into your own life so that your life will be a shining example to others."

Dennis Bentley – When Mark said you were going to live in a caravan, something quickened in my spirit that the Lord dropped into my heart earlier on during the praise time and it is this – He wants you to learn something, and learning it will take time, but by the grace of God let it be quickly and it is this. The normal Christian life is living our lives and going to God, going into his presence for help but God wants you to live in his presence like John in Revelation, caught up into his presence. To learn to live in his presence and come out from there and witness, and serve and minister and communicate the love, and the grace and the glory of God to others. It is not going to be easy. It is going to take time. It is going to take patience, but the Lord is calling you up so that you live with him in that caravan. You won't be lonely. You will be alone with

God and abide in his presence and come out from there in power, in power. You are unique so keep your uniqueness, do not become like the rest of us. Be yourself, because God has his hand on your life and abiding in his presence you will find your place. The years that have gone by have shaped you. Now God is going to reshape you, but you are going to be unique, boy. The blessing of God on your life is going to be great so be patient, be patient, because it is going to happen. Now remember, learn not to go into his presence for help but learn to live in his presence and come out and minister to others, then go back into his presence.

Pete Robinson. Unlike Mark, I didn't prepare anything this morning, but just as we were praying a little bit earlier, I just felt God drop something in my mind by way of a picture – just about his keeping power. If you plant a rambling rose, it's not very long before you need to put a stake in the ground beside that rose for it to climb up. The longer that the stake is there, and the longer that the rose climbs, the harder it is to separate the two. You cannot take the stake away can you? It just grows and grows and together they become very strong and the great thing about a rose is it's not like other flowers. It has thorns, and those thorns are there to protect it from what ever comes at it, and I just felt God saying to me that in that picture you are like the stake and he is like the rambling rose and what he wants to do is to climb around you and together you both become strong. What God is saying is "Don't keep moving the stake. The more you keep moving the stake, it is going to be very hard for me to grow around you to create that dual strength". So God is saying, "Put the stake in the ground and allow the rambling rose that I am, to grow around you and together we will become strong." And God says, "It will not just be strong in the ground but it will be strong enough to ward off that which will attack us." I just feel God saying, very much in my heart, that he wants to grow around you more and more and to anchor you into him. So together with Him you will become strong, and you will be able to ward off that which will come against you. The other great thing about rambling roses is that they live a very long time. You may live a very long time, and God says, "Let us grow together that you might have long life strong, true, able to ward off the enemy and just be able to be that which is beautiful". Because when roses bloom they are very beautiful, and you forget about the fact that you can cut yourself when you grab hold of them, but they look beautiful, and God says "Together we will be strong, but we will be beautiful".

Tim Bilson – Isn't it interesting how God says the same thing through lots of different people? It says in Revelation "He who has an ear let him hear what the spirit says to the churches. To him who overcomes I will give some of the hidden manna. I will also give him a white stone with a new name written on it known only to him who receives it." (Revelation 2:17)

And the hidden manna is something of the provision of God – I think what it is, is something for you to discover, but it is something of the provision of God. The white stone, to me, is a token, a token of the right to come into the presence of the King as a son. That passport, that ticket, whatever it will be, that token says you can come in to the presence of the King, whenever you want. So there, as a token of what God's got for you, is a white stone which says "come in to the presence of the King whenever you want, you have a right to be here."

Celia Bentley. – Just a scripture for you Bobby. "Just as you have received Christ Jesus as Lord, continue to live in him, rooted and built up in him, strengthened in the faith as you were taught, and overflowing with thankfulness. See to it that no one takes you captive through hollow and deceptive philosophy, which depends on human tradition and the basic principles of this world rather than on Christ. For in Christ all the fullness of the Deity lives in bodily form, and you have been given fullness in Christ, who is the head over every power and authority. In him you were also circumcised in the putting off of the sinful nature. Not with a circumcision done by the hands of men, but with the circumcision done by Christ, having been buried with him in baptism and raised with him through your faith in the power of God who raised him from the dead.

When you were dead in your sins and in the uncircumcision of your sinful nature, God made you alive with Christ. He forgave you all your sins, having cancelled the written code that was against you, with its regulations that was against you and that stood opposed to you; he took it away, nailing it to the cross. And having disarmed the powers and authorities that were against you, he made a public spectacle of them, triumphing over them by the cross". (Colossians 2:6-15)

And what I had this morning was that you are part of the triumphal train of Christ. One of the first fruits as we all are, who are believers. When Jesus died on the cross, he took captivity, everything that captivates and captures us and holds us in bondage, he took it and made it his own captive so that we can be free and we are part of the triumphal procession that comes behind Jesus, as his brothers and sisters, as the first fruits of what he died on the cross for and you are part of that this morning. You are part of the triumphal procession of Jesus.

Ellen Burgess – Father I just want to thank you for Bobby. We love having him in our family and you love him and we love him. Father I just pray for him that he will be like a tree by a river – a tree with deep, deep roots and that, even when it is dry, it will be rich inside, that his life will be green and fertile. Father I just pray that he wouldn't play around, now that he has found you, now he's decided Lord that he would be sold out for you. We see people come into the Kingdom, like one foot in and then one foot out – Lord that he would be someone who is sold out for you.

Lord I see him like a David, someone who is passionate, someone that is passionate for you, and also someone who is motivated by passion. Not someone who is worried about what other people think or feel but Father, someone who is sold out and motivated by his love. Father I pray that his life would be marked by your friendship, that he would be known as a man who is a friend of God. Father I thank you for all his talents. I thank you for all that he is, and I pray that you would take all those things that you have put in him, and those things that you have planned before the beginning, that you would take all those things, and that you would channel them into your plan and your purpose for him and that you would call him to be a man of great compassion. Lord that he would cry with your tears and that he would know the secrets of your heart, and that he would drink deep in your love. Father, I just pray that he would be a channel of your love, a channel of your compassion and that Lord he would be a communicator. Lord I pray that he would communicate with all the things you have given him, all the talents, that he would communicate your love and your heart and your passion and your friendship to others.

EPILOGUE

MY FRIEND

As you can see from reading this book I am now in the grip of a gentle giant, meaning the Lord Jesus Christ, where I am happy to be. I have found my friend. God bless you all.

For info on Book
or musical concert bookings
go to: -
www.journey2freedom.co.uk

Contact mobile number :
07506 797272